OUTDOORS
ONLINE

An Internet
Guide to
Everything
Wild & Green

Erika Dillman

THE MOUNTAINEERS BOOKS

THE MOUNTAINEERS BOOKS
is the nonprofit publishing arm of The Mountaineers Club, an organization founded in 1906 and dedicated to the exploration, preservation, and enjoyment of outdoor and wilderness areas.

1001 SW Klickitat Way, Suite 201, Seattle, WA 98134

© 2007 by Erika Dillman

First edition, 2007

Manufactured in the United States of America

Copy Editor: Brenda Pittsley
Cover Design: Mayumi Thompson
Interior Design and Layout: Jennifer Shontz, Red Shoe Design
Cover photograph: © Royalty-Free/Corbis

Library of Congress Cataloging-in-Publication Data

Dillman, Erika.
   Outdoors online: the Internet guide to everything wild & green / Erika Dillman.—1st ed.
       p.   cm.
   Includes index.
   ISBN 1-59485-068-2
1. Outdoor recreation—Computer network resources. 2. Internet. I. Title.
GV191.6.D55 2007
796.5—dc22

                                                            2007003116

✿ Printed on recycled paper

CONTENTS

OUTDOORS ON SNOW

THINGS TO DO, PLACES TO GO

WILDLIFE

STAYING ALIVE

OUTDOOR COMMUNITY

STEWARDSHIP AND SUSTAINABLE LIVING

GEAR

INTRODUCTION

GET WILD & GREEN

You'd rather be hiking through an alpine meadow or kayaking in Baja—who wouldn't—but you have a job, or it's raining, or you broke your leg skiing and can't leave the house. During downtimes between adventures, why not get your outdoors fix online?

Outdoors Online: An Internet Guide to Everything Wild & Green is full of bookmark-worthy websites and blogs where you can find photo galleries of your favorite national parks, watch surfing and snowboarding videos, brush up on climbing techniques, swap gorp recipes with other campers, plan your next mountain biking trip, and research the latest gear. Step off the beaten path, and you can also discover new outdoor activities such as skateboarding with your dog, hiking in the buff, unicycling in the mountains, or running with the bulls in Pamplona. It's all here.

Personally, I like surfing the web so I can get inspired and live vicariously through other people's expeditions, treks, and exploits. I won't be climbing Mount Rainier or paddling the Northwest Passage any time soon (just because I write about outdoor and fitness topics doesn't mean I have the time or energy to push myself *that* hard). Hiking, mountain biking, and snowshoeing are more my style. But I'm open to new ideas. I'd never heard of geocaching before I started this book, and now I can't wait to go to my first cache hunt and plant a travel bug.

THE SITES

Obviously, the Internet is a vast resource, full of websites covering every imaginable—and unimaginable—subject. Zeroing in on the information you need can be time-consuming, even for a computer-savvy outdoors person like you. So I surfed for you. I put away my hiking skort, eschewed my own outdoor plans, and spent several months Googling and Yahooing my way around hundreds of outdoor sites and blogs, searching for useful, interesting, and entertaining content.

In the end, I chose sites I like (Wildernet, *www.wildernet.com*), sites I love (Treehugger, *www.treehugger.com*), sites that made me laugh (The Biker Fox, *www.bikerfox.com*), sites with mind-blowing action and nature photos (*Alpinist* magazine, *www.alpinist.com*), sites with inspiring stories, ideas, or events (Grays on Trays, *http://graysontrays.com*, and The Rock and Ice Ultra, *www.rockandiceultra.com*), sites that might offend some people (you be the judge), sites I think are important (Survive Outdoors, *www.surviveoutdoors.com)*, and a few sites only people under twenty-five could enjoy (*Method* magazine, *www.methodmag.com*, and *Snowboard* magazine, *www.snowboard-mag.com*).

I also included sites and blogs hosted by government agencies, guiding companies, journalists, bike commuters, environmental magazines, competitive athletes, novices, and a few odd folks who dare to dream...or who simply have too much time on their hands.

HOW TO USE THIS BOOK

Nature isn't tidy, and neither is this book. Just as you cross paths with wild critters and spot rare flowers in the woods, in this book you'll find all sorts of interrelated tidbits as you ramble through each Wild & Green category. You'll find safety information in the hiking section, hiking information in the safety section, and volunteer opportunities everywhere. Remember, it's the journey that matters. If you're looking for a specific subject, check the index for sites covering that topic. Chances are, there's more than one.

As you know, sometimes websites change their look and content, bloggers stop blogging, and links that used to link stop linking or send you to a 404 Error page. Since so many of the sites listed here are from established organizations, you shouldn't have too many misses.

Finally...just in case you need reminding: you cannot really learn how to climb a mountain or kayak class 3 rapids from reading a book, magazine, or website, and you shouldn't really believe everything you read, either. Bloggers aren't always qualified to instruct, journalists can make mistakes, and even the experts sometimes give conflicting advice. Use the sites in this book to get started, but always seek professional instruction or guidance before heading into the wild.

Have fun. Be safe. Leave No Trace.

THE GREAT OUTDOORS

Climb the mountains and get their good tidings. Nature's peace will flow into you as sunshine flows into trees. The winds will blow their own freshness into you, and the storms their energy, while cares will drop off like autumn leaves.

— John Muir

1 GET OUTSIDE GUIDES

ONE STOP SHOPPING
http://gorp.away.com

If you only visit one site, make it this one. GORP, *Outside* magazine, and the travel portal Away have joined forces to bring you the Mall of America of outdoor websites. Say you want to go rock climbing. Whether you're a beginner or a seasoned adventure junkie, you'll find everything you need here to make it happen. Start by reading skills articles and searching for a local class or guide. Next, learn a few essential climbing knots, and ask the Gear Guy what to wear. When you're good to go, read destinations pieces on top climbing spots, such as Joshua Tree, Arches, and other national parks. Finally, click to the travel section to book your ticket. The site has hundreds of articles, as well as discussion boards, on every imaginable outdoor activity.

ALL ABOUT ADVENTURE
www.about.com

What about cycling? Or running, walking, skiing, or surfing? Whatever your game, About.com has the activity covered and provides links to other topical sites as well. Article topics range from getting started how-tos to specifics such as what to do when your bike blows a tube and which sites to surf for the latest wave forecasts. The text-only format is a bit dry, and it's a bit irritating when the links open inside the About framework, but the information comes in small, easily digestible bites with enough subtopics to give you the whole picture.

THE ABCs OF OUTDOOR SPORTS
www.maxlifestyle.net

Their "Maximizing Lifestyles" tagline may sound like a condom brand slogan, but the producers behind this recreation guide get it right in the details. The site (it's actually a network of twelve sites, each offering the ABCs of a popular outdoor activity) is professional and comprehensive, providing background, planning, and technique information in organized, bulleted points. It does a thorough job of explaining the whys behind apparel and equipment selection, essential skills and techniques, and health and safety tips. Search for guides and outfitters; plan and book trips; read the latest outdoor news stories; shop for ski boots, soft shell jackets, and more. Some of the topics on this site are also available in Dutch. Bonus.

GO PLAY
www.getoutdoors.com

I thought I wouldn't like GetOutdoors—the interface seemed too clean and clinical—but I was won over by a video of a cougar chasing a grizzly bear. Then I stuck around and visited the site blog, GoBlog, and found a breathtaking photo of someone walking a slackline between two mountains and a post describing furniture made of recycled bicycle tires.

The GoLearn section is a convenient resource for short and accessible adventure- and skills-related articles, covering topics such as ice climbing tools, camping cuisine, health and safety, single- vs. double-wall tents, soft shell jackets, woman-specific gear, and the basics of belay devices. For bare-bones details, you can search for destinations by state, country, activity, and terrain, and then click to one of sixty-nine outdoor outfitters to plan your trip. Go travel.

2 OUTDOOR MAGAZINES AND VIDEOS

LIVIN' LARGE

www.stellarmag.com

Continuous snow reports from around the world, a kayak lingo lesson, interviews with pro rock climbers, an artist who specializes in trout paintings, and the co-inventor of bungee jumping—Stellar is adventure news without the hype. Get news feeds on competitive skiing, cycling, and surfing, and on U.S. teams, pros, and events. Curious about heli biking in Canada or thru-hiking in New England? Stellar's the place to learn more. Watch action trailers of adventure movies or full-length webumentaries. Visit the Community section to chat with others, post a blog or photos, and enter contests to win free gear.

SO MUCH MORE THAN KERMIT

www.pbs.org

Unless you've been living under a boulder for the past several decades, you're probably familiar with PBS (the Public Broadcasting System, home of *Sesame Street* and *Masterpiece Theater*). But have you checked their website lately? Follow Jean-Michel Cousteau's *Ocean Adventures*, in full gorgeous color and sound. Observe monk seals on a remote Hawaiian beach, or swim alongside JM when he comes face-to-face with a great white shark in the South Pacific. Trace migrating whales on a colorful interactive map, and watch a pod of orcas attack a gray whale and her calf—bummer, but that's nature—in a narrated slideshow. Also, read expedition diaries and download both audio and video podcasts. Speaking of *Nature*, don't miss this show's online videos, episode previews, interviews, articles, and photos of penguins, pandas, lizards, lions, and more. Search the Critter Guide for facts on your favorite animals. Games and puzzles for the kids. History and science programming for you.

THE WORLD ON YOUR SCREEN
www.nationalgeographic.com/ngm

You thought the magazine was engaging? Try the website. National Geographic, Interactive Edition, offers a similar mix of natural phenomena and cultural commentary, brought to life with audio and video clips narrated by researchers, scientists, and explorers.

Sit back and watch a photographer explore underground white-water rapids (with fall-in-the-river-and-you-die turbulence) in a New Guinea cave system; follow arctic polar bears via a live webcam; or review the archives for full multimedia coverage of 500,000 sandhill cranes on their spring break in Nebraska. (You can't really know a sandhill crane until you've heard its croaky, cooing call.) Click over to other NG publications such as *Adventure*, *Traveler*, and *Expeditions* for more.

Then study the Adventurer's Handbook, a free online guide with thirty-six pages of "Crucial Skills, Nifty Tips, and Shameless Shortcuts" filled with wonderfully illustrated survival strategies as well as tips on beaching a kayak, wiping out on a bike, avoiding an avalanche, swinging a machete, and other critical outdoor skills. If you still need more, the site has the requisite epostcards, downloadable wallpaper, and polls, forums, and contests.

OUTDOORS
ON FOOT

Above all, do not lose your desire to walk: every day I walk myself into a state of well-being and walk away from every illness....

— Søren Kierkegaard

3 WALKING

WALK THIS WAY

www.thewalkingsite.com

It's so simple: Put one foot in front of the other. Repeat. But you want more. You want to burn calories, you want to change your diet, and you want advice on workout planning. The Walking Site is an excellent starting point for walkers of all levels. You'll find stretching and strength training exercises, walking and marathon training programs, nutritional guidance (complete with a calorie calculator!), and to keep you motivated, lots of friendly support on the message board. Find clubs and additional training information (from Prevention.com and other reliable sources) on the links page.

WALK LIKE A SCANDINAVIAN

www.inwa.nordicwalking.com

www.nordicwalkingnewsblog.blogspot.com

Scandinavians have been pumping up their power walks with walking poles for decades. Isn't it time you got more bang for your buck? Check out The International Nordic Walking Association for detailed instructions on nordic walking techniques, illustrated warm-up and cooldown exercises, and a brief but thorough guide to pole selection. Click to the North American site to find an instructor in your area. For a more personal touch, head to British instructor David Downer's Nordic Walking News blog where you'll find technique tips, articles, industry news, event reports, and more.

MEDA WALKING

www.wildmind.org/meditation/walking
www.contemplativemind.org/practices/subnav/walking.htm
http://yogateacher.com/text/meditation/on-line/walking.html

Slow down, pay attention. Walk your way into awareness. Walking meditation is more and less than exercise and scenery; it's mindfulness at your
feet. Learn about the practice at the Wild Mind Buddhist Meditation
site, and then visit The Center for Contemplative Mind in Society's site for
instructions. Check out Texas yoga teacher Charles MacInerney's site
for more instructions and a reminder to "smile with every cell of your
body." I'm feeling more relaxed already.

FEET, DON'T FAIL ME NOW

www.vonhof.typepad.com/happy_feet

Anyone who walks, hikes, or runs knows about foot pain. Lucky for us,
John Vonhof, author of *Fixing Your Feet: Prevention and Treatment for
Athletes*, cares enough to share his expertise on keeping our dogs happy.
Start with the scary blister photos (see how yours compare), then search
his blog for posts on skin and nail care, shoe-fitting tips, purchasing
orthotics, and simple foot stretches. There are also links to websites of
"must-have" foot care products, such as BodyGlide and Engo patches,
and sock manufacturers. Sorry, you'll have to buy the book if you want
the treatments.

DISCOVERING AMERICA

www.walkingthestates.com

Brits Dave Toolan and Stuart Hamilton make walking across the country
(a 5000-mile coast-to-coast trek via the American Discovery Trail) seem
almost easy. In spite of blisters and Achilles tendon injuries, the threat of
crossing paths with an escaped convict, and a sandwich-stealing cat, their
trail journals and photo gallery are filled with amusing and thoughtful
observations. It's no wonder they make so many friends along the way. As if
their adventures weren't inspiring enough, I loved reading about the songs
running through Stuart's head and iPod at various stages of the journey.
To name a few, Marvyn Gaye's "What's Happening Brother?," Wilco's

"Candy Floss," and Carly Simon's "You're So Vain." Well designed and well written, this site is one of my favorites. Follow them through 2007.

THE JOURNEY OF 1000 MILES...
www.thefatmanwalking.com

Follow "Fat Man" Steve Vaught's struggle to lose weight and jump start his life by walking across America. His existential ramblings from his 2005–2006 trek are sometimes painful to read, but it's worth walking in his shoes for a while. Most journeys aren't glamorous or historically important; the important thing is to keep moving...and try not to lose your mind.

WORLD WALKER
http://home.earthlink.net/~earthwalker1

In 1970, Dave Kunst left Waseca, Minnesota, to walk around the world with his brother, John, and a pack mule named Willie Makeit. Along the way, they met Princess Grace, Thor Heyerdahl, and a camel driver who wanted to trade his ride for Willie. Kunst left the trek after his brother was killed in Afghanistan, then restarted four months later. In 1974, he walked back into Waseca, becoming the first person to circumambulate the Earth on foot. It's old news, but still an engaging story.

KEEP ON WALKIN'
www.walkingman.org

If you see a man walking down the street pushing a jogging stroller filled with camping gear, it just might be Gary "Walkingman" Hause. As of late 2006, Hause was walking almost thirty miles a day, spending less than $40 a week on food, and was fifteen thousand miles and almost halfway through his walk around the world. Surviving on oatmeal and the occasional pizza, Hause has dodged vultures, communed with buffalo, survived a puppy bite, and met plenty of Good Samaritans offering food, assistance, and money. His good-spirited journals are fun to read. There's also a color cartoon strip of his journey. You can see it all, though, in Hause's Flash movie, a two-plus minute slideshow accompanied by the Proclaimers' song, "500 miles." Talk about a quick link.

DIRTY SOLE SOCIETY
www.barefooters.org

I never knew kicking off my shoes was such a big deal, but apparently there are folks out there who feel oppressed by the shoe-clad majority. I expected this site to extol the pleasures of walking through fresh cut grass and feeling beach sand sift and squish between your toes, that sort of stuff…and there's a bit of that. But the barefoot walkers, runners, and hikers of the Society for Barefoot Living are on a mission to go "barefoot pretty much everywhere, all the time, as a lifestyle choice." The site provides information on state laws allowing bare feet in public places, a database of barefoot-friendly stores and restaurants, and a printable liability waiver to give to property owners who might expect you to wear shoes for your own good. The society also organizes quarterly hiking outings and other events. You're welcome to join them—just leave your shoes at home.

CITY WALKER
www.newyorkcitywalk.com

Some adventurers collect peaks or rivers; some walk the mean streets of the city. New Yorker Caleb Smith walked all over Manhattan Island, visiting every neighborhood and covering seven hundred miles during several years of weekend walking. His photo gallery is a showcase of New York City history, architecture, and culture. There are crumbling stairways and facades, the old Macy's stables, the Holland Tunnel ventilator shafts, cathedrals, a spooky photo of Charles Lane at night, rare sightings of Louis Sullivan and Frank Lloyd Wright buildings (actually, one of each), the Fulton Fish Market, turtles in a Central Park pond, the Roosevelt Island tram, and that's not even half of it. Follow Caleb for a while, and see New York like you never have before.

4 ORIENTEERING AND GEOCACHING

WALKING FOR NERDS

www.chicago-orienteering.org
www.us.orienteering.org
www.gaorienteering.org
www.floridaorienteering.org

Don't you ever get tired of just walking and walking? Step it up and add the challenge of finding your way by compass. Start at the Chicago Orienteering Club's site for answers to basic questions, then visit the U.S. Orienteering Federation's site for introductory information, a national club directory, event schedules, race results (yes, it's a sport as well as a recreational activity), a list of equipment suppliers, and links to related sites. For a more detailed approach, read the Georgia Orienteering Club's illustrated Beginner's Guide and Florida Orienteering's online tutorial for explanations and illustrations of checkpoints, control descriptions, and punch cards. Visit Kimbo's geocaching page to see photos of actual cache logbook entries *(www.guysnamedkim.com/geocache)*.

GET ORIENTED

www.learn-orienteering.org

Kjetil Kjernsmo's the man. A Norwegian graduate student and an orienteering enthusiast, his illustrated guide, "How to Use a Compass," is a must-see site for budding orienteers. Kjernsmo's instructions are as easy to navigate as finding north on a compass. Stay on course, and you'll learn how to use a compass and map to get yourself wherever you want to go. The site also includes tips for orienteering in foggy conditions, practice exercises, and instructions for finding your way when you're mapless, compassless, and completely lost.

And just for fun, go to Kjernsmo's personal website to hear an audio clip of him pronouncing his name. Cool.

WALK THE TALK
www.orienteeringunlimited.com/visualglossary.htm
www.orienteering.org
If you're going to walk the walk, you need to talk the talk. Learn the lingo at Orienteering Unlimited, and study the symbols at the International Orienteering Federation's site.

HIGH-TECH HIDE-N-SEEK
www.geocaching.com
www.terracaching.com
www.navicache.com

Are you a hider or a seeker? Or both? Do you know where your travel bug is now? Navigate your way to Geocaching, the source for all things caching, including a searchable worldwide database of cache locations, news and events, and getting started information. Thousands of cachers participate in the site's forum, sharing tips, ideas, and photos of cache treasures. If you're thinking, "geo-what?" here's how it works: Using a GPS unit and a set of coordinates, people search for caches, hidden containers holding wooden or foreign coins, plastic action figures, or other useless but often amusing treats. When they find a cache, seekers leave new treasures, as well as short notes in the cache logbook. Add the thrill of the hunt to your walks and hikes. You never know when you might find a five-pence coin or a Pokémon trading card. Search similar sites, TerraCache *(www.terracaching.com)* and Navicache *(www.navicache.com)*, for more cache locations.

MONKEY MADNESS
www.monkeycache.com

What if you found one of those red hanging monkeys from the Barrel of Monkeys game in a cache somewhere in the woods, and you took it from its cache and dropped it off in another cache, maybe even in a cache in another state? Of course, you'd email the red monkey guys at Monkey Cache with that monkey's serial number so they could track its location. But then what if someone *else* found that monkey, and took it to Spain, and emailed the red monkey guys? And so on, and so on, and so on. What a barrel of fun. The monkeys are loose; help track them. (If you get tired of monkeying around, check out the little green army soldiers deployed around the word at *www.geocachearmy.com.*)

WHEREVER YOU GO, THERE YOU ARE

www.confluence.org

You haven't really been "there" until you've posted your coordinates. For example, take 41°N 98°W, a soybean field in Hamilton, Nebraska, or 43°N 118°W, a sagebrush- and cowpie-covered desert in Malheur, Oregon. Thanks to the Degree Confluence project, GPS-armed adventurers have a place to post photos and descriptions of their journeys to confluence points around the world. (FYI, a confluence point is an intersection between specific degrees of latitude and longitude.) Of course, it's not about the destination but the journey, so make sure you read the trip entries to see otherwise meaningless coordinates transformed into personal adventures. According to the site, there are 64,442 confluence points, with thousands still waiting to be logged. What are you waiting for?

I'D RATHER BE CACHING

www.miragee.blogspot.com

It's not enough to find almost two thousand caches—Miragee also blogs about them. His entries are fun to read, with enough detail to keep you interested, photos to set the scene, and enthusiasm that's downright contagious. His Something to Think About sidebar quotes are sort of corny ("If you find happiness, people may be jealous. Be happy anyway."), but seem totally appropriate for his site. With links to GPS reviews, useful software, and other geobloggers.

GEOLAUGHING

www.geocities.com/cacheinon

For a good laugh, browse the features section of Huntnlady's geocaching site, where she describes her idea for a geocaching *Seinfeld* episode. Then share urban geocaching stealth techniques with other cachers, brush up on your geocaching survival skills, or cuddle up with your laptop and spend some quality time on the geocaching haiku page. If you're really bored (or really into it), try coming up with your own reasons "why Geocaching is like sex."

GEO OKIE
http://gpsokie.blogspot.com

GPSOkie isn't just a taker. He puts a lot of thought into the items he leaves in caches—usually foreign coins because he knows kids get a kick out of finding them. Visit his blog for articles on caching tools, posts on cache hunts, and nature photography. If you have any questions about geocaching, you'll find more than you need on GPSOkie's blogroll, which links to all the important caching sites and blogs.

CACHE IN, TRASH OUT
www.cacheintrashout.org

Next time you head off on a woodland, beach, or mountain cache hunt, or on any outdoor outing, for that matter, bring a trash bag. Better yet, organize a Cache In, Trash Out (CITO) event to clean up trails in need. Check the site's FAQ page and upcoming events link for basic information, and discuss cache and trash issues with other cachers in the forum.

CACHING FOR EVERYONE
www.handicaching.com

Don't let accessibility concerns keep you from seeking your hidden treasure. At the Handicaching site, you can find locations that work best for you. Caches are rated on accessibility based on five variables: distance to cache, route surface, route slope, route obstructions, and cache height. The site also posts brief personal essays from cachers who have used the system, general caching news stories, and links to geocaching sites around the world.

5 RUNNING

HAL ONLINE
www.halhigdon.com

There may be no better online running source than Hal Higdon's site. In the past fifty years, he's competed in hundreds of distance races, coached cross-country teams, and designed training programs for runners of all abilities. For most of that time, he's also written for *Runner's World* magazine and cranked out several dozen running books. His site is packed with articles on every running topic, from pacing, to nutrition, to injury prevention. Don't take anyone else's advice; follow his training programs (which he generously posts for free) for every distance from 5K to ultra marathon.

NOT JUST A WALK IN THE PARK
www.trailrunnermag.com

In the Javelina Jundred, a 100-mile race through the Arizona desert, the playing field between men and women is pretty darned level. Women can win the race. That particular race report is one reason to visit *Trail Runner* magazine online. A few other reasons: destination articles on the best running trails in Zion National Park, New Hampshire's White Mountains, Las Vegas, and the Canadian Rockies; training advice for snowshoe racing; tips on running with your dog; what to eat on the run; and trail-tested reviews of hydration packs, running shoes, and LED headlamps.

RUNNING INTO THIN AIR

www.skyrunner.com

For some people, trail running isn't just a pleasant jog through the woods; it's a grueling endurance event such as the Pikes Peak Ascent. The starting line is 6200 feet above sea level, and the finish line is 13.2 miles straight up, with a 7815-foot gain. If you can survive that, they'll let you sign up for the marathon next year. Read the finishers' "learn before you burn" quotes and race reports for all the ugly details. Skyrunner also provides training tips on running at altitude, race results, links to local running clubs, and information about Colorado mountain races and training spots.

RUN FOR ALL

www.coolrunning.com

Cool Running is a valuable resource for all types of runners. You'll find training advice for all distances from experts such as Jeff Galloway, as well as racing strategies and event-specific training schedules and work-outs. Search the Races/Results section for trail, mountain, road, track, and multisport races around the country. There's a free online mileage log, plus pace and calorie calculators. Connect with other runners over thousands of forum topics, and check out reader-submitted personal essays at the Community pages. Visit the Running Blog Family Directory *(http://completerunning.com/running-blogs)* for links to nearly a thousand running-related blogs.

ULTRA CRAZY
www.run100s.com

I love running, but I draw the line at 100-mile races. Who wants to be on their feet for 14 hours? Apparently, lots of ultra runners. Luckily for them, Run 100s has information on dozens of North American mega races, a calendar of events, a list of ultra clubs, and a lot of race photos for inspiration. If you're a glutton for punishment, read yearly reports from the Leadville 100, the Superior Trail 100, the Vermont 100, and more than three hundred other ultra events. You'll also find links to clubs and to other running websites and blogs. Check out Scott Dunlap's and Sam Musleh's blogs *(http://runtrails.blogspot.com; www.ultrablog.us)* for an inside look at the sport.

6 HIKING

SGT ROCK'S BASIC TRAINING

http://hikinghq.net

Don't be offended by the "dirtbag sissies" comment that graced the home page when I visited; SGT Rock's Hiking H.Q. is worth a read. Yes, he's a real Army sergeant, and he's all about "hiking your own hike," keeping it simple, and leaving no trace. He'll tell you how to prevent monkey butt, how to outfit yourself with a fifteen-pound pack for less than $300, and how to hike at night without a headlamp. There are also book reviews, a few gear reviews (brands you probably haven't heard of if you're used to buying fancy gear), trail journals, and a friendly forum for hiking discussions and tip sharing. SGT Rock is one of the few hiker advice-givers to extol the virtues of wool as a base layer, so he gets my vote for that. He'll be hiking the Appalachian Trail in 2007. Stay tuned.

HIKE LIKE MIKE

www.hikingwithmike.com

If you're new to hiking, or just want some guidance, spend a few minutes at Mike's site reviewing his tips page. Leader of the Zion Wilderness Survival School in Utah and author of *The Complete Hiking, Backpacking and Wilderness Survival Manual*, Mike's hiking, backpacking, and camping tips will keep you comfortable and safe. Maybe you already know not to run away from a bear, but did you know that perfume, hair products, and deodorant can attract bears? Do you know what to do if you get lost? Mike does. Plus, what to put in your pack, how to prevent and treat bug bites, and so much more. The site is pretty basic designwise, and the information isn't always separated into tidy categories, but the details are in the right place. Dog owners will want to read the section on hiking with dogs.

CONNECT THE BLOGS
www.tommangan.net/twoheeldrive

If you were only allowed to visit one hiking blog, it should be Tom Mangan's Two-Heel Drive. No esoteric or sappy nature ramblings here; just newsy, topical information. Mangan keeps his entries brief, adding just the right balance of reader feedback to energize and personalize the site. His main focus is sharing the broad range of sites and blogs he finds interesting, edifying, inspirational, and sometimes, just silly. If not for him, you might never learn about a blind hiker's successful six-day backpacking trip, or ponder the preponderance of portable phones on public pathways, or know where to find an online pee-bottle discussion, or read about the thirty-one different ways to tie your shoes, or know what a woodpecker-pecked tree looks like. Two-Heel Drive has one of the best hiking blogrolls I've seen. Visit his home page, Busy Being Born *(www .tommangan.net),* for weekly trail journals and photos.

THE SCHLONG AND WINDING TRAIL
http://wanr.earthbiz.net/NWminiguide.html
http://wanr.earthbiz.net/StevesHiking.html

No joke; there's a man named Dick in Washington State who has a website detailing his nude hikes in the Cascade Mountains. He's happy to share fifty-seven of his favorite hikes, marking those trails where he's been seen all nekked—just in case you're thinking of scampering through the hills in the buff and want to know how to avoid (or encounter) those prudish clothed hikers (aka "textiles"). Actually, Dick is only one of many who contribute to the Western Association for Naturist Recreation's website. Click around the site to read about women-only outings near Los Angeles and about Steven's ("HikingNude: The Reactions!") all-natural adventures (yes, there's shrinkage). But wait! There's more! At Nude Hiking in the Yukon and Alaska *(www.yukonalaska.com/nudehiking),* you can read naturism articles, connect with other nude hikers, and bone up on nudism etiquette. Finally, for a full-frontal entrée to the sport, visit Roger's

Nude Hiking home page *(http://internettrash.com/users/natural/hiking .html)*. Or not. (Be forewarned….Fig leaves not included.)

WATERSIDE ATTRACTIONS

It's not like you need a reason to hike, but sometimes knowing there's a treat at the end or along the way makes the journey that much sweeter. The **Swimming Holes** *(www.swimmingholes .org)* site lists more than nine hundred swimming holes, hot springs, and waterfalls across the country, plus some basic water safety tips. If you just want a hot soak, visit **Hot Springs Enthusiast** *(www.hotspringsenthusiast.com)*, where you can search for hot springs by location, GPS coordinates, water temperature, and USGS quadrangle. The **Soakers Bible** *(www .soakersbible.com/index.asp)* is a more polished site with photos and descriptions of hot spring locations, as well as contact information for nearby lodgings and great links to maps, soaking etiquette, and spa sites. Check out **Soak** *(www.soak.net)* for a well-attended forum, reports and photos of soaks around the world, and a searchable database of hot springs. Finally, the **National Geophysical Data Center** can tell you where to find every recorded hot spot (there are 1661 to date) in the United States: *www.ngdc.noaa.gov/nndc/servlet/ShowDatasets?dataset =100006&search_look=1&display_look=1.*

YOUR OWN OUTDOOR DUDE

www.outdoorsdudes.com

If you can't trust a dude, who can you trust? Emergency Dude has survived earthquakes, lightning storms, heat waves, and droughts. Water Dude has been safely drinking from natural water sources for years. Compass Dude knows his way around a map. But the dude I love most is Hiking Dude because he has one of the most comprehensive, easy-to-read hiking sites I've found. He covers every important topic—from training for and planning trips, to packing instructions and checklists, to trail etiquette and safety. He knows what to do if you get lost, encounter a bear, or get a blister. He's a real live mountain man, so he also knows about river cross-ings and about hiking in altitude, cold weather, and desert conditions. Hiking Dude knows what's best for you, and he has a calorie counter! What's not to love?

PACK A SALTY SNACK
www.toddshikingguide.com

Start with the Warning! page of Todd's Desert Hiking Guide for a reminder that desert hikes can lead to "exhaustion, heat stroke, and death." Rattlesnakes are the least of your worries. Good preparation, a bag of Cheetos (for the salt), and enough water should get you through the day. Where to go? Todd has thoughtfully described, in splendid detail, more than one hundred Arizona hikes (and a few in Utah and Colorado as well). Each entry includes a brief summary, driving directions, hike length and difficulty, required skills, and road conditions, along with substantial step-by-step trail reports and a few photos. He also rates hikes and suggests relevant books and maps.

ALL ABOUT YOU
http://besthike.com/blog

Whenever anyone says "best" about anything, I'm usually skeptical. So when I came across the Best Hike blog, I expected to find some snotty, hyperactive, Gore-Texed adventure boy, bragging about all his super exciting trips, as if people who haven't hiked the Pacific Crest Trail just don't cut it. I was *so* wrong. I love this site! It's not about *him*; it's about all the cool sites he finds for *you*. The host hardly says a word; his posts mostly consist of short introductions to various outdoor topics, followed by excerpted articles, news information, or personal trail journals from other sites and blogs. Never boring, the Best Hike blogger always in-cludes amazing photographs and colorful maps, lots of alpine-related topics, gear info, plus posts on coastal hikes, scrambles, multi-day hikes, and safety. (PS If you want details on specific hikes, check the mother site *http://besthike.com*. Not as much fun, but useful.)

7 BACKPACKING

ARCTREK 1000
www.ryanjordan.com

In the summer of 2006, Ryan Jordan, cofounder and publisher of *Backpacking Light* magazine, and two friends walked a thousand kilometers across the Alaskan bush and tundra in twenty-four days. Brutal! Staying true to their ultralight roots, they used the lightest gear available. Their trekking essentials accounted for only seven pounds of their fifty- to sixty-pound packs; the rest was food. Share the adventure, the foot pain, and the fear at Arctic 1000. For more on backpacking light, gear advice, and trip photos, visit Jordan's Backcountry blog *(www.ryanjordan.com/weblog)*.

YOU'VE GOT FRIENDS
www.thebackpacker.com/trailtalk

If you're considering a January trip to Death Valley or wondering where to hike in Florida, consider posting a few questions on the Trail Talk forum at The Backpacker. Somebody will send you a link to photos from his trip, somebody else will share advice on bug sprays, another somebody will direct you to a local hiking organization, and then somebody new will chime in correcting the previous advice, while yet still somebody else will issue a warning about trolls. (Trolls? Hey, it's an open forum; you take what you get.) Anyway, there are thousands of threads in this forum; it looks overwhelming, but you can search for your favorite topic to narrow down the list. If you want more, there are smatterings of how-to articles, personal essays, trail reports, and plenty of user comments on gear.

HAPPY TRAILS TO YOU
www.adventurematters.com

I know, it's *so* been done before. Someone takes a little plastic devil doll or a cheerful gnome or a goofy bobblehead on vacation, and then posts dozens of photos on her website of said doll in places a doll would never go on its own. At first I hated Griswold the Traveling Gnome at Adventure Matters. But then I found a photo of him outside Chicago's Field Museum, standing next to a dead squirrel fives times his size. It made me laugh, so I gave the site a chance. Adventure Matters is written by Kimberly, an avid hiker eager to share her love for the outdoors. She's done an admirable job of assembling a range of useful and inspiring content (even if some of it is a bit corny), including trail lessons, trips reports, a long list of U.S. trails (in alphabetical order, thank you), her favorite books, and links to other informational and personal web pages.

SOME TELL IT, SOME SELL IT
Here are some nature photos you won't want to miss:

www.snow-nymph.com

http://blog.paulsveda.com

http://rockymountainscenery.com

www.pbase.com/jwalk/root

40 MEGS OF FUN
http://members.aol.com/cmorhiker/backpack

There's an insane amount of backpacking and hiking information (along with side orders of paddling and cycling) on Chuck's Backpacking Bonanza. Chuck's been everywhere, from the Palmetto Trail in South Carolina to the Trail of the Coeur d'Alenes in Idaho, and he has trip reports to prove it. He also shares his tips, favorite literary quotations, reading list, his original backcountry poetry, and photos of elk, bison, deer, and caribou. Extras include links to conservation and government organizations. Nice work, Chuck!

LIGHTEN UP
www.backpackinglight.com

Don't take less; just take lighter stuff. At Backpacking Light you'll find detailed cross-reference charts comparing lightweight stoves, carbon fiber hiking poles, and featherweight tents. You'll have to subscribe to the site (or to the print magazine) to read full text staff-written reviews. Bummer. Still, you can visit the G Spot (it does exist!) forum for community posts on sleeping bag insulation, hand-crank pumps, and hat debates (full brim vs. baseball cap). The site also contains reader-submitted mini reviews and few useful freebies, such as gear checklists for packrafting, backpacking, and winter backpacking and camping.

ALL YOU NEED TO KNOW
www.backpacker.com

It's not all about peak bagging and thru-hiking at *Backpacker* magazine. It's also about new gorp recipes, foot care, learning how to use an altimeter, and staying dry on the trail. Experts are on hand to answer your gear and technique questions, and thousands of other backpackers are waiting to meet you in the forum. The Backpacker site has comprehensive trip preparation advice and maps for the Appalachian, Pacific Crest, and Continental Divide trails, as well as articles and trip reports on day hike destinations such as Lake D'Arbonne State Park in Louisiana and Sky Meadows State Park in Washington, D.C. Set up your own outdoor profile, and keep a log of miles hiked, nights bagged, and elevation gained. Bonus: they have a specialty Guide for Outdoor Women and an impressive wilderness Survival List.

8 CLIMBING AND MOUNTAINEERING

LEARN THE ROPES

www.tradgirl.com
www.planetmountain.com
www.chockstone.org
http://climbing.tropic.org.uk

If you don't want to plummet to your death, you'll pay attention. Beginners should start with TradGirl, a basic text site with articles and a long list of FAQs on buying gear, training, ice climbing, and other topics. Planet Mountain's mountain guides offer instruction on climbing techniques such as ice belays, abseiling, and single-pitch rope maneuvers. There's also expedition news, climbing articles, and gear reviews. Chockstone, an Australian climbing site, has a lot of photo-illustrated technique tips. At the Archive of Climbing Moves, you'll find articles for beginning climbers, rack and rope buying advice, and several illustrated technique and skills tips.

TERMS TO TRAINING

www.spadout.com

How's your rack? Analyze it with the Rack Simulator at Spadout to find out what you need (or don't need) for your next climb. This outdoors wiki and forum has basic and intermediate instruction on backpacking, climbing, caving, and skiing. Learn the lingo, view and post adventure photos, read interviews with outdoor experts, scout trip locations, study photography techniques, and get in shape with training strategies. You can research backpacks, snowshoes, and countless other products using their gear comparison chart (which, of course, includes one-click shopping links).

THE CLIMBING LIFE
www.alpinist.com

When I see pictures of people climbing rock faces zillions of feet above the ground, or worse, hanging from rock faces in little hammocks, I think "That is just not for me." Same goes for climbing those giant icicles. I'd rather live. Still, I couldn't help looking at *Alpinist* magazine. More artsy than outdoorsy (*Alpinist* magazine even hosts its own film festival), this elegant site features first-person accounts from climbers around the world. There are also features stories, profiles—of climbers and of mountains—and breaking climbing news, all illustrated with amazing photos. Climbing isn't my thing, but reading about it is another story.

CLIMBING FREE
http://lynnhillclimbs.com

Okay, I spoke too soon (The Climbing Life, above); I do like climbing. In fact, I fell in love with it and with free climb star Lynn Hill about four paragraphs into climber John Long's loving introduction to Hill's book, *Climbing Free: My Life in the Vertical World.* Read it for yourself, and check out Hill's article, "The Essence of Technique," and you'll be in love with this down-to-earth diva, too. Hill leads climbing camps (featuring organic gourmet meals) in Texas, West Virginia, and Sardinia, among other locations. For a real treat, watch a short climbing video showcasing Hill's effortless style. Visit her blog for trip reports, photos, and climbing podcasts.

BUTT SHOTS AND BOULDERING
www.climbing.com

Every month on the *Climbing* magazine site, there's a new butt shot. (It's not what you think.) There's also news from local and worldwide walls and crags, photo galleries and videos of climbing events, and all you want to know about gear. The tech tips—for alpine, sport, big wall, ice, bouldering, and trad—are friendly and illustrated with amusing cartoons. Features include articles on alpine multi-pitch moderates in Utah, bouldering in Bolivia, and climbing at the Hetch Hetchy Reservoir in California, as well as an events calendar, a forum, and pro blogs. For more news, blogs, and route info, also check Rock Climbing *(http://rockclimbing.com)*.

A POUND OF PREVENTION
www.mountainsafety.org.nz

The more adventure blogs you read, the more you hear about accidents and death. So do your homework before you go. At the New Zealand Mountain Safety Council site you can download instructional and safety pamphlets, as well as research papers, on traveling in the bush, snow sports and avalanche issues, radio communications, and river safety information. They also offer outdoor courses and leadership training.

MEMBERSHIP HAS ITS PRIVILEGES
www.americanalpineclub.org

Join the American Alpine Club, and you'll have access to The Grand Teton Climbers' Ranch in Grand Teton National Park, as well as discounted rates at bunkhouses and cabins in Wyoming, Colorado, Oregon, New York, and other states. If you really know your way around a mountain, you can apply for AAC endorsement of your next expedition, which basically means you'll have an easier time crossing borders and finding sponsors. The AAC also offers grants to individual climbers.

GO CLIMB A TREE
www.dancingwithtrees.com

It's not just for kids anymore. We can all climb trees! It'll take half a day, though, because these are no ordinary backyard trees. Georgia-based Dancing With Trees offers tree climbing and camping programs for kids and adults—Girl Scouts can even earn their tree climbing merit badges here. The Pacific Tree Climbing Institute *(http://pacifictreeclimbing.com)* in Eugene, Oregon, also offers guided tree climbing adventures. Choose from day climbs, moonlight climbs, and tree camping. There's even a five-day family tree climbing camp.

THE AIR DOWN THERE

www.caves.com

http://cavingintro.net

www.caves.org

Sure, alpine vistas are breathtaking and white-water rapids are exhilarating, but don't forget that there's a whole world down under just waiting to be explored. Caves are cool and damp and a little spooky in a magical sort of way. Plus, you get to wear a headlamp. What could be more fun? Mine the Caves website for in-depth resources on underground exploits. Download PDF files of current and past issues of *Cavediggers* magazine; join discussion groups on caving, cave surveying, cave rescue, cave biology, and other topics; and study cave stats. The site contains illustrated instructional articles on rigging equipment and caving knots, as well as hundreds of links to introductory information *(www.cavingintro .net)*, caving clubs around the world, caving videos, virtual cave tours, a National Geographic slideshow on the Chiquibul cave system in Central American, and cave locations. Don't miss the links to web galleries for some fascinating cave photos and to the National Speleological Society's site *(www.caves.org)*, where you can learn more about caves and download brochures and booklets on responsible caving, lava tube caves, and bats.

FOLLOW THE LEADER

www.traditionalmountaineering.org

How long is *your* ice ax? See if it measures up at Traditional Mountaineering, where novices and advanced alpinists go for free mountaineering advice and instruction. Hosted by Oregonian Bob Spiek, founder of the Cascades Mountaineers Alpine Climbing Club, former chair of the Sierra Club's Angeles Mountaineering Training Committee, and Search and Rescue volunteer, the site covers every imaginable mountain topic including preclimb meals, rappelling devices, snow caves, avoiding avalanches, and boot and pack selection. Learn (or review) the ethics and guidelines for leading or participating in a group climb; download emergency kit checklists, a sample climb prospectus, sign-in and incident report forms, and other essential planning tools; and read about a few pros, such as alpine-style purist Steve House and mountaineering legend Reinhold Messner. The site also contains up-to-date posts on Bend, OR, weather conditions, local classes on backcountry skills, national climbing news, reader-submitted trip reports and photos, and an exceptional links page. From here, click to photo galleries, mountaineering organizations and clubs, expedition sites, microbreweries, and additional inspiring and instructional adventures sites.

PLAY IT SAFE
www.avalanche.org

Pull your head out of the snow. If you're going to play in the mountains, you need to learn about avalanches. The WestWide Avalanche Network is packed with essential avalanche resources. Start with the FAQs page for basic information, then click on Education for links to an online tutorial, state avalanche centers, and the American Avalanche Association's home page, where you can read excerpts from *Snow, Weather, and Avalanches: Observational Guidelines for Avalanche Programs in the United States*, link to additional avalanche resources, and download snow symbol fonts. If that's not enough, the WWAN has dozens of research papers and other safety guidelines in its library; links to conferences, journals, and research organizations; information on avalanche dogs; a photo gallery; and a job board.

KNOT TILL YOU'VE TIED OFF
Learn essential climbing knots here:
> www.climbing.ie/knotstop.html
> www.jpmountainguide.com/climbing-knots.html
> www.virtualinks.com/index.htm
> www.realknots.com

WHEN IN DOUBT, ASK A GUIDE
www.acmgguides.com

Of course you can't learn how to climb a mountain by reading a website, but you can start learning about essential skills. The Association of Canadian Mountain Guides has a colorful, well-organized site with a general mountain guide. There are illustrated articles on glacier travel, roping, crevasse rescues, map datum, decision making, anchors, rappel devices, and snow fleas. You can find even more information on the community pages, where guides answer reader-submitted questions on mountaineering, skiing, ice climbing, avalanches, and guide training.

OUTDOORS
ON WHEELS

Don't be afraid of going fast and getting hurt. (You can always wear black stockings to cover up the scars!) You just have to forget what your parents taught you—stuff like being careful, looking good, and catching the best man available.

— Marla Streb

9 MOUNTAIN BIKING

WHERE TO RIDE

www.bikeride.com

Looking for a cyclo-cross race in New York? Or a 150-mile bike tour in California? Maybe a mountain bike series in North Carolina? Whether you ride on the street, trail, or track, you'll find plenty of places to ride on Bike Ride. Check out upcoming events, search the database for events in your state, or add an event. While you're at it, scan the left margin for world racing news headlines.

GET THE DIRT HERE

www.dirtragmag.com

Why subscribe when you can get the dirt for free? Read the latest mountain biking news at Fresh Dirt, ponder staffers' musings on the two-wheeled lifestyle at Brain Farts, and drool over bike porn. Dirt Rag also features product reviews, articles (check out New Zealand's best single-track trails), pro interviews, and a literary contest for mountain bikers. Take time to view the photo and art gallery (check out artist Kevin Nierman's funny profile and bike paintings), and stop by the forum to talk shop (or politics) or to hook up with other riders. There's a women-only forum as well as a general category where mountain bikers talk about their other interests—books, music, and film. Finally, visit the extensive links page for gear, clubs, travel companies, other bike media, events, and more.

COME ON AND TAKE A FREE RIDE
www.nsmb.com

You've gotta love a site that has a "Pimped Rides and Gear" category in its photo gallery and a nine-page, 121-post-long thread on dough heads and freetards in its forum. North Shore Mountain Biking is *the* webstop for, by, and about freeriders. These high-energy guys give a whole new meaning to "Look, Ma, no hands," with amazing photos of people on bikes flying through the air—upside down, right side up, sideways, seated, unseated, and hands-free. Plus reader-submitted Trail Tales, reviews of trick gear, race coverage, and pro interviews. Check out up-and-coming talent in the Bros Not Pros brofiles section. (Sorry, Grrrls, there are only a few articles in the Chicks Not Dicks section.) Buy, trade, or sell bike parts, plan rides, and watch other riders' videos at the massive forum. Rad.

WHERE YOU WANT TO BE
www.dirtworld.com

Start with the Dirty Stories (in the Trail Guides section)—"Busted at Pot Peak," "Fresh Fruita," and "Hairballing Down Mt. Fuji"—for your fill of epic ride reports. But if you just want the dirt on great rides throughout the U.S., use the Dirt World database, searchable by type, trail, or location. Think your favorite trails are shred-worthy? Post'em on the site. There's some coverage of pro riders and a few site links, but Dirt World is focused on showing and telling readers the best places to ride. There's also plenty of industry news—some staff written, some from other magazines or organizations. Plus race and event announcements and coverage, gear reviews by staff and readers, and tips 'n' tricks. If you're looking for a riding buddy (or another kind of buddy), click on Hotties or Buddies. Have fun. Get Dirty.

FAT TIRE HISTORY
www.mtnbikehalloffame.com

Did the military have the idea first? Was it a group of young Parisians with too much time on their hands? Or maybe it was the inventor of the "Woodsie Bike"? The Mountain Bike Hall of Fame says, thanks for the input, guys, but it really all began in Northern California in the 1970s with a ragtag band of fat-tire cyclists called the Cupertino Riders. Follow their story to the first Pearl Pass tour, then to the Repack Road race in Marin County. Click on the link to Repack race founder Charlie Kelly's site *(http://www.sonic.net/~ckelly/Seekay)* for a walk through his personal scrapbook of 1970s mountain biking culture. To be fair, don't take the Hall of Fame's word on everything: an essay on the High On Adventure site *(http://highonadventure.com/Hoa97aug/Montana/montana.htm)* provides photographic proof that infantrymen in the late 1800s rode through the Montana wilderness on what look suspiciously like early versions of mountain bikes. That should count!

WANTED: MOUNTAIN BIKERS
Get paid to ride all day; check out *www.mountainbikingjobs.com*. Maybe you'd rather lead kayaking trips, teach skiing, or manage a conservation program. For more outdoor jobs, visit: **Job Monkey** *(www.jobmonkey.com)*, the **Outdoor Adventure Professional Network** *(www.oapn.net)*, **Cool Works** *(www.coolworks.com)*, Eco Jobs *(www.ecojobs.com)*, and **Outdoor Industry Jobs** *(www.outdoorindustryjobs.com)*.

RIDE FREE OR DIE
www.mountainbikemilitia.com
Members of the Mountainbike Militiamen Movement are armed and ready for war—with anyone who gets in the way of a great ride. If a "bastard landowner" blocks access to a great ride, they say, "Blow up his car." If a bike company claims a certain high-priced frame is bulletproof, they say it's merely "bullet resistant." They know because they took it outside and blasted it with sixty rounds. The gun-toting bikers behind this green and khaki site are either really funny or really scary. You decide. Either way, you might want the T-shirt.

SAVE THE SINGLE TRACKS
www.imba.com
If you missed one or all of the International Mountain Bike Association's epic ride celebrations, don't despair. You can see slideshows of each and

every one on the IMBA site. The site is really geared toward land and event managers, but riders should take a look. Read about the trail crews who make your rides possible, and pay attention to forest policies or land development that could threaten your favorite rides.

GET A FIX

www.utahmountainbiking.com

Is your chain lubed? Is your Camelbak clean? If not, take a look at Utah Mountain Biking's online Fix It repair manual. Complete with color photos and step-by-step instructions, this handy site will have you tuning your brakes and mud-proofing your cables in no time. When you're finished, click to the main page for Utah trail descriptions and photos, articles on resistance training and tubeless tires, and free screensavers and mountain biking videos. In case you need reminding, scan the injury index for treatments for blisters, bleeding, nail avulsion, fractures, dog and snake bites, foreign bodies, heat stroke, and more.

10 CYCLING

EVERYTHING ON TWO WHEELS
www.bicycling.com

Get it all here, no matter what type of bike you ride. The website for *Bicycling* magazine has training and racing advice, pro profiles, fix-it and maintenance tips, industry news, product reviews, race results, and upcoming North American events, as well as a searchable database of the best rides in one hundred U.S. cities. Watch skills videos, calculate calories burned, join thousands of cyclists in the forum to share epic rides, find a cycling partner, mull over Tour de France controversies, or discuss the books you're reading while your broken bones mend. No subscription required!

THE BIKER FOX ROCKS
www.bikerfox.com

Trendsetter, bike stuntman, fitness enthusiast, sexiest man of the year… yep, that's the Biker Fox. I LOL at his wacky and wonderful website, and you will, too. The loveable Fox looks like a cross between Weird Al Yankovic, sans mustache, and the elf king from *The Lord of the Rings* and channels Pee Wee Herman on steroids. Watch hilarious videos of the Fox shakin' his groove thang, flip through his "Fashion Trend Setter" and "Fashion Trend Guru" photo albums, and listen to messages fans have left on his answering machine. There's more: click to his business site, Billions and Trillions, Inc., to buy 50s and 60s muscle car parts.

BOTTLENECK BIKING
www.critical-mass.org

Just show up and ride. Hopefully, in large enough numbers to stop traffic—car traffic, that is. Critical Mass doesn't have an official website, but you can check this unofficial site for a list of more than two hundred North American cities (most with site links) and dozens of international cities with Critical Mass activities.

Visit Michael Bluejay's Critical Mass site *(www.critical-mass.info)* for details, resources, cycling links, energy and pollution information, and even incident reports about bad cops harassing good cyclists at CM events.

For fun, click over to Screed *(www.scorcher.org/screed)*, and download images various groups have used to advertise their events and views. My personal faves: a Pee Wee Herman poster and Parking Clown decals you can slap on cars parked in the bike lane! Pick up more "properganda" at CICLE (Cyclists Inciting Change Thru Live Exchange), and spread the word. PS You'll want the T-shirt and a pack of "Women of the Velorution" stickers *(www.cicle.org)*.

THE JOY OF CYCLING
www.jimlangley.net

You should have to pay to view Jim Langley's Bicycle Aficionado website. With a *Farmer's Almanac* feel and dozens of vintage cycle illustrations, photos, and magazine ads, this labor-of-love "cyclopedia" of bike history is also the best place to learn every aspect of bike care and repair—not to mention a few "stupid bike tricks." Langley's friendly style makes it easy to follow along whether he's writing about his cycling memorabilia collection, profiling the many bikes he's owned and tested, or explaining how to solve "numb bum." A former technical editor for *Bicycling* magazine, Langley can fix anything on any bike; his repair instructions (always illustrated with drawings or, in some cases, video clips) are stellar. Bookmark this one; you'll want to keep coming back for more.

LIFE IN THE BIKE LANE
www.kenkifer.com

It's no surprise that dozens (I stopped counting at 150) of cycling, outdoor, and travel sites link to Ken Kifer's Bike Pages. Kifer, who was hit and killed by a drunk driver in 2003 while riding near his home, was a regular guy who loved Thoreau and cycling and wasn't above writing a few cycling fairy tales. His site, now maintained by his best friend, is designed and organized for easy navigation, with the perfect balance of humor, how-to, and personal stories. You won't find action photos or testosterone-laced raves here, but articles on touring with a solar-powered computer, bike camping, and health and fitness programs. If you want to get serious, there are some stats and surveys on hand, as well as advocacy and commuter information.

TAKE A BITE OUT OF CRIME
www.nationalbikeregistry.com
If you love your bike, learn how to lock it. Meanwhile, the National Bike Registry is taking a bite out of bike theft through a national registry. According to the NBR, many stolen bikes are actually found but wind up in police auctions because they aren't registered. For $10, you can add your bike's serial number to the national database for ten years. You never know. You might be one of the lucky ones.

TALK, TALK, TALK
www.bikeforums.net
www.cyclingforums.com
What do cyclists do when they're not on their bikes? Probably work, eat, and sleep. But they definitely talk to other cyclists, too. Bike Forums and Cycling Forums both draw thousands of participants and cover most of the same topics, such as training tips, race and event information, mountain biking, and finding rides and riding partners. Bike Forums also has posts on folding and tandem bikes, distance touring, masters cycling, and tips for car-free living. Registration is required to view Cycling Forums' photo galleries, safety posts, unicycle discussions, and women-specific categories.

RULES OF THE ROAD
www.bicyclinglife.com
Bicycling Life is dedicated to keeping everyday cyclists safe. Here you'll find a bike safety quiz, several articles on bike commuting and advocacy

strategies, and an illustrated guide to traffic rules. The site also provides a link to a state-by-state listing of U.S. cycling laws. Review the skills section to brush up on the basics, such as making left turns, navigating intersections, and avoiding road hazards. There's also a bike repair section, where you can email experts Crank and Hub with fix-it questions. Bicycling Life has an extensive links page, connecting you to regional cycling clubs, advocacy and commuting organizations, bike repair guides, and other related sites.

BIKE COMMUTING 101
www.runmuki.com/commute
Thinking about bike commuting? Visit Paul Dorn's site. He's a former pack-a-day smoker who took up cycling and hasn't looked back. Dorn does a terrific job outlining in simple terms the most important elements of bike commuting, such as route planning, carrying capacity, and basic bike maintenance. He'll also help you overcome your fear of flat tires and direct you to information on keeping your work clothes wrinkle-free.

BIKE COMMUTING 202
www.commutebybike.com
This simple, attractive blog makes bike commuting an appealing option. Well organized, with just enough color and a sprinkling of photos and video clips, Commute By Bike makes it easy to get from a post on using a bike trailer for large-haul errands, to a profile of the Commuter of the Month, to a post about finding the right bike (durable but disposable) for the Burning Man festival *(www.burningman.com)*. The posts and articles are never preachy or smug, but inquisitive, informative, and casually inspiring. The site includes reviews of apparel, nutrition bars, bikes, and accessories, as well as awesome links to other cycling blogs and sites. Check out the Driver's Pledge at Bike Traffic *(www.biketraffic.org/content .php?id=60_0_11_0)*.

PUNKS ON BIKES
www.carsrcoffins.com
I was so ready to get all punk rock about the Cars-R-Coffins ezine. Break some stuff, steal a bike, lash out at those selfish SUV-driving gas hogs.

Now I just want their T-shirt with the wheeled coffin logo on the chest. All sorts of cycling bloggers link to this site, but I'm not really seeing "the action" or the attitude they promise. One cool Iggy Pop quote and an anemic three-post blog just don't do justice to this stark, dark site's graphic energy. They're working on a new site design, so let's hope there's more content (and plenty of chaos) to come.

A THIRD SOCK

http://mudhead.uottawa.ca/~pete/bike.html

"Frostbite of the penis is not funny," says Canadian bike commuter Peter Hickey. His solution: a third sock. Hickey makes no bones about the fact that he's not a cyclist; he just rides to get to work in cold (15°F and above), very cold (0 to 15°F), extreme cold (–15°F to 0), and insanely cold (below –15°F) weather. And he does it on a $25 ten-speed he found at a garage sale! His "pedal till you get there" philosophy and fondness for Sorel boots make his minimal site as refreshing as a cool blast of snow in the face.

BIG BIKE CLUB

www.cascade.org

According to the Seattle-based Cascade Bicycle Club, they're the largest recreational cycling club in the United States, with more than 6000 members. They produce several cycling events (including the STP, a two-day, 200-mile ride from Seattle to Portland), organize 1300 daily rides in the Puget Sound area, and provide links to cycling routes in the region. Through its education foundation (*www.cbcef.org*), the CBC offers free and low-cost clinics on techniques and bike maintenance, and promotes bike safety and bike commuting. The site also has downloadable brochures on helmet fitting, cycling in traffic, and other useful topics.

BIKES ON ICE

www.bikewinter.org

You could sit around and mope about the windchill factor, or you could quit your whining and join the winter velorution. The first item on the Chicago-based Bike Winter site's list of winter biking essentials: willingness. That's just the Midwestern way, as is getting together for a hot dish and a few beers after a ride. Check out the Icicle Bicycle Festival and the Baby Doll Polka Club ride in Chicago, the Santa Cycle Rampage in Milwaukee (the latter includes links to a G-rated nude Santa and hilarious subversive anti-Santa rants that have nothing to do with cycling; *www .santarchy.com*), or a winter cycling skills workshop in Ann Arbor. The site has resources and tips on everything from what to wear to handling skills, plus links to other useful winter biking sites.

FRIGID FREEWAY
If you think your winter bike commute is bad, trying riding 1000 kilometers across the Arctic Circle: *http://bikeforest.com/arctic.*

BLIZZARD BIKING
www.icebike.org
Recreational, competitive, and commuting cyclists will find all the information they need about winter biking at Ice Bike. Whether you're a novice looking for inspiration or a veteran ice biker seeking validation, you'll enjoy reading some uplifting personal stories about cycling the Iditarod Trail or commuting in a New York blizzard. Before heading out on your own rides, visit the section on calculating windchill factor, and review black ice vs. deep snow techniques, then heed the advice on selecting footwear, base layers, mittens, and more. Don't forget about hydration!

11 UNICYCLING

MUNI MADNESS
www.unicycling.com

What could be more fun than clowning around on a unicycle? Municycling! As in mountain unicycling. Unicycling expert John "the Uni-Cyclone" Foss's personal website is loaded with hundreds of action and nature photos from group rides and muni events in and around California. See municyclers riding across fallen trees and gigantic boulders, and climbing hills that would be challenging on two wheels (or two feet)! Foss also includes a brief intro to the sport and gear and equipment tips. Don't miss his "Things Not to Do on a Unicycle" page. Seriously.

BIG WHEEL KEEP ON TURNING
www.unicycling.org
www.unicyclist.com

Find your balance at The Unicycle Page, a hub of unicycling resources. Start with the "You Rode Where?" section to see unicyclists parasailing, riding around the South Pole, bungee jumping, and pedaling through mud; study the International Unicycling Federation's 10 skill levels; and learn fancy tricks to entertain your friends. Unicyclist Community *(www.unicyclist.com)* provides links to unicycling events and communities around the world (check out clubs in Sweden, German, and New Zealand), as well as to multimedia sites featuring unicycling videos. Hang out at the 13,000-member-strong forum to share favorite rides, read about upcoming events, learn techniques, and talk gear with unicyclists around the world. You can post in English, Dutch, German, and Finnish.

Finally, visit The Unicycle Blog *(www.unicyclist.org/blog)* for unicycling trivia and more than 3000 videos.

HAVE WHEEL, WILL TRAVEL
www.adventureunicyclist.com

New Zealand adventure and mountain unicyclist Ken Looi has covered a lot of ground, unitrekking in Nepal, municycling in a 900-kilometer tour of the Swiss Alps, competing in dozens of races around the world, and unicycling more than 500 kilometers from Vietnam to Cambodia to raise money for OXFAM. Looi holds a Guinness world record for unicycling 378 kilometers in twenty-four hours and even graduated from medical school riding a unicycle under his cap and gown. His event and race logs are sweet and funny, and his photo albums make me want to get a unicycle and head for the hills. A simple, charming site.

DO NOT TRY THIS AT HOLM
www.krisholm.com

Visit mountain unicycling world champion Kris Holm's site, and you'll see a photo of him hopping from one boulder to another across a mountain stream. *On his unicycle.* Then click to his photo gallery and have your mind blown. There's Kris in the forest jumping from one rickety wooden platform to another. There's Kris hopping down incredibly steep red rock with an immense canyon below. There's Kris peddling along the handrails of a wire bridge over a roaring river. There's Kris flying through the air between two tower-like rock formations (the type you see in car commercials where there's just feet of space between life and death). The site also features descriptions of Kris's videos, an info page about the different types of unicycling, and a catalog of Kris Holm brand unicycles and accessories.

CONCRETE CAPERS
www.insane.unicyclist.com

"Life is pain" is the Insane Unicyclist Gang's motto. Their website looks pretty cool, all gritty and urban, but isn't up to full speed yet. Coming soon: a photo gallery and riders' bios, and most important, more videos. For now, check out Motorama Competition 2003, a brisk, boppy clip of riders hopping and jumping their way through an indoor obstacle course to the soundtrack of Goldfinger's "Superman." There's also Funkadelic Wheel-jam 2004 and Miguel's Jalapeno Adventure. I guess I'm not cool enough to know if a "four-foot-double-triple-pineapple-banana" is an actual unicycle maneuver or just some uni trash talk, but I heard it on one their videos. You figure it out.

OUTDOORS ON WATER

The rivers are our brothers. They quench our thirst. The rivers carry our canoes and feed our children. If we sell you our land, you must remember, and teach your children, that the rivers are our brothers and yours, and you must henceforth give the rivers the kindness you would give any brother.

— Chief Sealth

12 KAYAKING AND CANOEING

A RIVER RUNS THROUGH IT
www.canoekayak.com

Are you a class 4 junkie, or more of a scenic paddler? You can be both at *Canoe & Kayak* magazine's website. Read about lobster fishing by kayak, communing with alligators and lizards in the swamps of the Okefenokee National Wildlife Preserve in Georgia, and ratcheting up the adrenaline in Washington's Green River Gorge. There are destination articles and photos to make you drool, plus inspirational stories of people who are crazy enough to canoe to the Arctic or smart enough to ditch the winter blahs for a kayaking retreat in Belize. Also, updates on white-water events, industry news and race reports, how-to articles, gear guides, and a small section on white water. Visit the Rivers, Tides, and Currents page for links to some of the best resources on tides, river flows, and other water conditions.

PADDLE TO PADDLE
www.paddling.net

Paddling is another great all-purpose site for canoeing and kayaking tips, paddling directories, trip reports, and links to paddling magazines and associations. There are articles on portaging, canoeing in wind, and common white-water canoe mistakes. In the kayak section: preventing shoulder injuries, rolling techniques, and how to punch through surf. And those are just the techniques sections. Paddling also provides illustrated articles on canoe and kayak parts, paddle recommendations, boat and gear buying guides, signaling techniques, and abs exercises, as well as reader-submitted product reviews, new product announcements, and quick links for shopping, swapping, sharing, and selling. Want more? See event listings, trip outfitters, and schools.

GO WITH THE FLOW

www.wavelengthmagazine.com

Discover hidden beaches on the Sea of Cortez, explore New Zealand's marine reserves, and learn essential kayaking skills and strengthening routines at *WaveLength* magazine's website. Download PDF files of the print mag's current and past issues for free. Or click on Selected Articles for specific topics, including building canoes and kayaks, crisis and safety skills, sea otters, paddling picnics, and even personal essays. If you're looking for a paddling partner, you can add your name to the paddling list, which is searchable by state.

HIGH TIDE? LOW TIDE? KNOW BEFORE YOU GO

Up #$&* creek without a paddle is nobody's idea of a good day out, so check the water conditions before you go. The **U.S. Geological Survey Water Watch** site *(http://water.usgs.gov)* posts real-time water data on stream flows and lake tables. **American Whitewater** has a national database *(www.americanwhitewater .org)* of river charts, class ratings, levels, and descriptions of specific sections of river. **Salt Water Tides** *(www.saltwatertides .com)* gives sea paddlers a resource for checking tide times and heights, as well as sunrise, sunset, and moon times at specific bays, sounds, and other waterways. For worldwide tides, visit the University of South Carolina's interactive **Tide and Current Predictor** pages *(http://tbone.biol.sc.edu/tide)*.

SEA TO SHINING SEA

www.seakayakermag.com

You have to subscribe to *Sea Kayaker* magazine to read the kayak reviews and almost all of the articles, but there are still a few reasons for nonsubscribers to stop by their site, too. Every few months they post two or three articles online, usually on safety and technique topics, plus a feature story. Contemplate gel-coat repairs, review the forward sweep stroke, or enjoy one writer's personal account of paddling the Inside Passage. There's a cozy forum if you'd like to swap stories with other kayakers. You can also search for river trails and kayaking clubs, and download trip checklist and float plan forms (a smart step that too many paddlers neglect).

IT'S KNOT ENOUGH
www.animatedknots.com
A boat is not a toy. You need to be able to tie it up, tie it down, pack it, rack it, tow it, and stow it. Learn the best knots for every situation at Animated Knots by Grog. The site provides written instructions and video demonstrations for fourteen common boating knots, including the bowline, the figure eight, and the sheet bend. You'll also find dozens of knots used in climbing, fishing, search and rescue missions, and other outdoor activities. Don't miss the section on rope care and storage.

RIVER RUNNING
www.kayakmagazine.com
Any magazine with an article about cornboating (a sport involving a kayak, a pickup truck, and a cornfield) deserves a look. Get another laugh with an inside look at how truly unhelpful airline representatives can be when you're trying to make travel arrangements for your kayak. *Kayak* magazine "is pure whitewater," with news on events and popular paddlers (such as the Canadian kayaker who's also a porn star). It's most active during spring and summer months; in the meantime, there are plenty of useful links.

KAYAK ON THE MIND
www.kayakmind.com
If work or injuries are keeping you off the water (what else would?), visit Kayakmind and live vicariously. Read about top river play spots (Chile, anyone?), watch videos of freestyle competitions, and get the scoop on new creekers and play boats. If you think your air screws and helixes are ready for prime time (or hilariously not), read the article on videotaping, and send them your best shots. Reader-submitted articles are welcome, too. If

you like Kayakmind, you'll also like Playak *(www.playak.com)*, which has action videos, an extensive photo gallery, and a huge kayaking forum.

TALL TALES AND SALTY DOGS
www.seakayaker.com

Horseshoe crab orgies in New Jersey. Free hypnosis practices (!?). Exploring and gunkholing in Connecticut. Kayak surfing. It's all fair game for Bob and John, the kayakers behind this wacky little sea kayaking webzine, The Salty Dog. Bob is all about facts and tides and solitude; John manages the "tall tales" department. The salty dogs are based in New York City, so many of the destination articles cover East Coast paddling adventures. Thanks (I'm assuming) to Bob, you can learn more about cold water kayaking and navigating through commercial traffic. The rest of the site is up for grabs. Click around and eventually you'll land on the Dynamic Mind Training Trance Coach's website *(www.trancecoach.com)*. Maybe John is on to something?

KAYAK KNACK
www.kayakhelp.com

There's no Who We Are introduction here to confirm the site's paddling credentials, but Kayak Help seems to know its stuff, providing good basic kayaking information. Learn about folding kayaks, wooden kayaks, slalom kayaks, touring kayaks, and every kayak in between. Beginner and intermediate kayakers will appreciate the many instructional articles on paddling techniques such as the forward and reverse sweep strokes, the sculling draw, and the low brace turn. The site also includes safety and rescue articles and kayak buying advice, as well as links to a number of kayak partner sites. Thanks for the help, whoever you are!

WHATEVER FLOATS YOUR BOAT
www.acanet.org

There's more to paddling than canoeing and kayaking. There's also canoe poling, kayak polo, squirt boating, and white-water slalom racing, to name a few. Whether you're a beginner or a daredevil, you can find water trails, paddling clubs, and pro schools at the American Canoe Association. The site has articles on basic skills, selecting equipment, and trip planning, and you can download a free sixteen-page color Beginner's Guide. The ACA also has excellent safety information, also downloadable, in visually attractive, easy-to-read formats.

DIG THESE DUGOUTS
www.canoemuseum.net

What to do on a rainy day? Visit the Canadian Canoe Museum for an overview of Canada's canoeing heritage. Its colorful, well-designed site introduces Canada's native cultures and canoe history. Start with the Paddler Profiles section to read about artisan William (Morning Star) Commanda, who teaches traditional birch bark canoe building skills in Ottawa, and Victoria Jason, the first woman to kayak the Northwest Passage. If you want to know more about wooden and bark canoes or about the North American fur trade, there are bibliographies and weblinks for every topic, as well as resources for boat builders.

PADDLE IT FORWARD
www.americanrivers.org

You'll portage through gunk and stinging weeds and slippery rocks and swarms of bugs, but will you take action to protect America's endangered rivers? American Rivers has the news, facts, and training information you need to help care for local rivers, streams, and watersheds. The site features downloadable resource publications and toolkits on a variety of water care topics, including river restoration, hydropower dam reform, and floodplains. Send a prewritten message to Congress, and search for a conservation group in your area. The River Network (*www.rivernetwork .org*) also has a searchable database, with 3600 grassroots organizations listed. Check the River Smart section for specific actions you and your family can take to protect our waterways.

CANOE STORIES
www.canoestories.com

Nocturnal stalking frogs, moose run-ins, turkey vultures, jumping fish, prehistoric-looking plants, and cooing loons. You don't want to miss Canoe Stories' first-person accounts of group and solo canoeing in the wilds of Northern Minnesota and Ontario, Canada. A common thread runs through all the tales: no matter how bad the bugs and no matter how brutal the portages, everyone comes out happy, inspired, awed, and very tired.

> **PADDLING PRIMER**
> Brush up on Victorian era boating guidelines by reading *Practical Canoeing: A Treatise on the Management & Handling of Canoes*, published in 1883, at *www.friend.ly.net/~dadadata /tiphys/Practical_1.hmtl*.

ROCK AND ROLL
www.kayakwisconsin.net

I feel a little guilty that I didn't read much of the Kayak Wisconsin blog, but I couldn't help it—I got distracted by the photo galleries. There are incredible photos of kayakers exploring sea caves in what I assumed was some exotic location. Nope, just Lake Superior (so I guess that makes them "lake caves"). Then there are the videos of kayakers demonstrating rolling techniques. And fact sheets on hypothermia, wind speed conversion tables, and kayak nomenclature. Basically, this site is packed with useful information for anyone interested in kayaking in Wisconsin—and beyond. Don't stop here: Kayak Wisconsin is a portal to more fantastic paddling sites and blogs, as well as kayak associations and specific kayaking destination sites. Get a few sites into this blogroll, and you'll realize that there might be many people out there having more fun than you are.

KAYAK NEW YORK
www.frogma.blogspot.com

Kayaking is fun, but it's not my life. That's why I like Frogma, a kayaking blog that's more about observing the environment than tricked-out boats and intimidating aerials. New York-based blogger Bonnie posts stories about the dead umbrellas she encounters on the way to the tugboat races, a gigantic flower at the Brooklyn Botanical Garden that gives a whole new meaning to the expression "man root," and her favorite paddles and sailing trips (photos always included). Follow her adventures via a virtual-tour photo gallery. Bonnie includes links to dozens of cool paddling, humor, and political sites and blogs, too.

PICTURE PADDLES
www.paddletales.blogspot.com

If paddling is a "silent sport," Paddle Tales blogger Peggy, a kayaker in north Florida, is the queen of stealth paddlers. Her trip photos capture, close-up and crisp, blue herons, green herons, preening egrets and flamingoes, playful river otters, a mother anhinga feeding her babies, and manatees floating just beneath the water's surface. Don't miss this field guide to Florida wildlife.

Or do you prefer cold weather kayaking? Visit Travels with Paddles *(www.seakayaker.nl/Journal)*, a blog posted by Dutch kayaking instructor Axel Schoevers, for engaging trip journals and captivating photos of dolphins, puffins, and grey seals.

13 SURF SPORTS

SURFING SEMINAR
www.surfing-waves.com

Learn how to paddle, duck dive, and catch a wave at Surfing Waves. Their beginners guide will help you select a board, prepare for your first wave, and talk like a real surfer. Gnarly! Get additional tips on lessons, tricks, travel, and waves at the site's forum. Surfing Waves also has articles on packing your board for airline travel, wave priority, and wetsuits. For a more comprehensive list of surfing lingo, browse Riptionary *(www.riptionary.com)*.

BREAKING WAVES
www.surfline.com

Get surf, weather, and wind forecasts and reports from your favorite beaches at Surfline. You have to be a subscriber to see the live cams and complete forecasts, but you can sign up for free "surf's up" cell phone alerts. The site also features surfing destination and travel articles, gorgeous slideshows, streaming videos, surfing news from around the world, and a women's section with tips, profiles, and videos. There's also a Surfology section, where you can learn the surfing Bill of Rights and Lefts, look up surfing terms, and ask other surfers for advice on treating surfer's ear. For more, visit WindGURU *(www.windguru.com)* and WaveWatch *(www.wavewatch.com)* for free surf and weather reports, including forecasts and wind, tide, and other important weather news.

SURF WITH THE PACK
www.wetdawg.com
Visit the Wet Dawg blog for a grab bag of wave and white water connections. Read about windsurfing in the Caribbean and kiteboarding in Cuba; watch wakeboarding, sea kayaking, and white water videos; and stay current on a variety of water events via news posts and live feeds. There are also links to a handful of pro blogs (worth a look), a photo gallery, and a small forum. See what the Dawgs have to say about GPS units, drysuits, water bottles, and other paddling gear in the reviews section. If you'd like some love with that hydration pack, check out the Hotties and Buddies sections, and get hooked up.

BARRELS OF FUN
www.surfermag.com
www.surferspath.com
Break out of your rut for a swell time surfing dozens of articles, thrilling photos, and worldwide wave reports at *Surfer* magazine's website. Watch videos and slideshows of pro events and top surfing spots, and submit your own. Also, download surf talk podcasts in the Live from the Pipeline section. The site also has a Surf Camp Guide, including links, contact information, and a comparison chart of your options. Share the fun and photos with other surfers in the forum (there are more than 75,000 threads in the general surfing category alone). Topics range from advice on ding repairs and getting rid of fleas to a discussion on whether George W. Bush would be a long- or short-boarder. For the most part, this is a guy magazine—just about the only place women appear is in the Bikini Betty gallery.

If you're looking for a mellower, but no less exciting, approach to fiberglass feats, visit Surfer's Path for links to awe-inspiring photo galleries and slideshows and to dozens of surfing sites.

SOUL SURFING
www.surfingrabbi.com
Join the Surfing Rabbi on his "kabbalistic quest for the soul." First, read "The Surf Rebel" for his backstory, then check out his Kosher Surf Camps in Mexico, Hawaii, Costa Rica, and Venice Beach. Visit the Newsletters

section (you have to subscribe to read them all) to "get spiritually stoked, Jewishly turned on, and open up your soul *(neshama)* to what Jewish Surfers International and Surf and Soul are all about." Groovy.

COUNSEL FOR BEACH DEFENSE
www.surfinglawyers.com

Some lawyers do their business on the golf course; others do it on the beach. The California-based Association of Surfing Lawyers is all about networking, as well as promoting ocean-based charities. Their site isn't particularly interesting or useful, unless you're looking for meeting and event schedules, but you should read its Surfer's Code and Surfer's Code of Ethics. You can also search the directory for a surfing lawyer.

WOMEN OF THE BOARD
www.legendarysurfers.com/blog

Unless you're a professional surfer or 15 years old, the web isn't the best place for women's surfing. So blow off the bikini sites and, instead, get stoked on women's surfing history at Macolm Gault-William's blog. Here you can read an excerpt from his book, *Legendary Surfers*, about outstanding "wood board women," such as Hawaii's surfing princesses Kaneamuna (mid-1600s) and Ka'uilani (late 1800s) and 1940's surf champion, Californian Mary Ann Hawkins. While you're there, check out his other free chapters for more on surfing culture and mythology. Aloha.

IT'S A SWELL LIFE
www.wetsand.com

I love WetSand because it's not surfy at all. In fact this sweet site looks and feels like a cross between a travel site and a conservation site. Read the surf, swell, and wave reports to find out the best time to surf in the Hinako Islands, Tahiti, or Panama. Take a look at surf art and photography, and get the latest headline news on shark scares and typhoons. Click to The Green Room for articles on the history of flip-flops and on making surfboards, an interview with Patagonia founder Yvon Chouinard, and photos of Buddy the Surf Dog *(http://surfdogbuddy.com)*. Another great reason to love this site: they have a women's surfing section where you can get all interactive with surfer-adventurer Liz Clark via an online journal, interviews, and video clips, as she sails around the world visiting the best surfing beaches.

DUDE, SAVE THE PLANET
www.surfrider.org

Surfers are people, too. And they care. With sixty chapters in the U.S., the Surfrider Foundation conducts public awareness campaigns, organizes beach cleanups, and gets all grassroots about protecting oceans and wetlands. Meanwhile, SurfAid International (*www.surfaidinternational.org*) sets up community health programs in the Mentawai Islands in West Sumatra and in the Nias Islands in North Sumatra. So what can you do? Organize a fundraiser, get out your checkbook, or take a garbage bag with you to the beach.

BLOGGING THE BIG WAVES
www.70percent.org

The 70 Percent blog has plenty of cool action photos and video clips, but it's not all fun and games. The blogger behind this site started taking water pollution seriously when a friend contracted meningitis after surfing a local break. So, before you start clicking around, add your own ocean-caused illness report to the site. The blog has posts on shaping, big waves, surf films, books, and general categories. Check Ten Links for Flat Spells for links to other blogs and forums. Sign up for the Waverider's Log to keep track of your sessions and breaks.

WINDY CITY SURFIN'
www.chicagokitesurfing.com

You don't have to live in paradise to kite surf; Chicago will do just fine. The Chicago Kitesurfing site is an excellent place to learn about the sport (also called kiteboarding), with a beginner's Q & A section, an explanation of kite dynamics, safety guidelines, a kiteboarding glossary, and illustrated fact sheets such as "Setting Up the Lines," "Cleat and Pulley Depower System," and "Slingshot Kiteboarding Surefire Wrist Release." Learn how to fix a leaky bladder, jump higher, and turn faster. Share stories, photos, and videos at the site's forum. For more details on kitesurfing techniques and tricks, visit Kite Surfing Now (*www.kitesurfingnow.com*).

GO FLY A KITE

Admit it. You've always wanted to be in pictures. Now's your chance. Answer the extreme sports video casting call posted on Kite Blog for your shot at fame. Then stick around and watch a few videos: How to Self Launch a Bow Kite, Snowkiting 101, or Kiteboarding's Original King of Air. Venture capitalist kiteblogger Chris's site *(www.kitevc.blogspot.com)* provides links to sites featuring Kiteflix and Kitepix, tricks, waterproof iPod cases, beach cams, and the Kite Forum *(www.kiteforum .com)*. Visit Kite Blog *(www.kiteblog.com)* for more videos and kitesurfing blogs. Don't miss The Kite Boarder blog and magazine *(www.thekiteboarder.com)*, where you can read real-time news, listen to podcasts, and download PDF files of the print magazine's destinations and feature articles, interviews with pros, video and gear reviews, and a free full-color kiteboarding manual.

THE CRUMPLE ZONE

www.boardlady.com

http://saucisseman.free.fr

Busted your board? No problem. The Board Lady can help. Click around the site of "the Queen of Fix" for lessons on board anatomy and checking your board for water, then visit Disasterpiece Theater for step-by-step fix-it photos for all types of boards. Maybe you'd rather build a new board. The site of the Saucisseman (that's sausageman in French) contains instructions for making a plywood and epoxy kiteboard, mounting a leash, and using the right knots. (It's only fair to let you know that his homemade board broke, so be safe and bookmark the Board Lady's site.)

CLOSE TO THE WIND

www.windcraft.com/windsurflesson.html

www.windsurfingbible.com/glossary.htm

If you're new to windsurfing (aka sailboarding), start at Wind Craft for an online windsurfing lesson written by master instructors. You'll learn the difference between kitesurfing and windsurfing, key safety tips, and board, boom, and mast basics. Visit the Windsurfing Bible for a comprehensive glossary.

UP IN THE AIR

www.americanwindsurfer.com/index.html

American Windsurfer magazine is one of those sites that pulls you in even if you've never tried the sport. Read about yoga poses for windsurfers, meet French windsurfing photographer Jerome Houyvet, and study "The Fine Art of Tacking." The site offers photo-illustrated technique lessons, access to many archived articles (don't miss "Profiles of a Windsurfer" and "Why I'm Not a Lawyer"), and gear reviews. You'll have to subscribe for complete access to current and past issues, but there's plenty to keep you busy for free. When you're ready to get on board, check out *Windsurfing* magazine *(www.windsurfingmag.com)* for intermediate ("The Longest Jibe") and advanced ("Bump & Jump: Aerial Off-the-Lip") instruction in text and Flash formats. (Coming soon: extreme instructions.) Stay tuned for the requisite videos, photos, board tests, and more.

OUTDOORS
ON SNOW

Powder snow is not fun. It's life, fully lived in a blaze of reality.

— Dolores LaChapelle

14 SNOW SKILLS

WEEKEND WONDERLANDS

www.winterfeelsgood.com

You can let your kids get fat in front of the TV this winter, or you can take them out and show them a good time. You'll find everything you need to get out in the snow at Winter Feels Good. This site is loaded with fact sheets on preparing for and participating in cross-country and alpine skiing, snowboarding, skate skiing, and snowshoeing. Learn basic skills and safety techniques, the difference between a green trail and a black trail, and how to select an instructor.

At Winter Trails *(www.wintertrails.org)*, you'll find a lot of the same info, as well as details on family-oriented snow sporting events across the United States and Canada. Just for teachers: downloadable curricula and instructions for including snow-sport instruction in physical education classes.

LET IT SNOW, LET IT SNOW

www.snowlink.com

Snowlink is a handy winter resource for anyone interested in learning about winter sports, with dozens of well-written articles about snowboarding, snowshoeing, and all types of skiing. A lot of the information here is similar to what you'll find at the Winter Feels Good site (above); both are part of the same cluster of sites sponsored by the Snowsports Industry of America. However, Snowlink has more content, such as articles on pre-season training, warming up and stretching, heli skiing and snowcat skiing, and airline luggage limits.

GET YOUR BUTT IN GEAR

There isn't really one site out there with comprehensive conditioning information, so you'll have to patch together a workout from a few sources. The **North American Ski Training Center** site *(www.skinastc.com)* has a great overview of the five basic principles of pre-season training. **Ski Home** *(www .ski-home.com/safety_info/snow_fitness.htm)* has cardio fitness tips, plus charts describing the best strengthening exercises for specific muscles and functions. Snowboarders can check out video clips of key snowboarding exercises at **Snowboard Secrets** *(www.snowboardsecrets.com/shapeup.htm)*. For a few more all-purpose winter sports exercises, visit **Active and Body Results** *(www.active.com/story.cfm?story_id=5110, www .bodyresults.com/S2Skiprep.asp)*.

KNOW THE CODE

www.nsaa.org/nsaa/safety/know_the_code.asp
www.skiontario.on.ca/code.asp

Before you strap on your skis or board, know the Responsibility Code. Read it at the National Ski Association, or visit the Ontario Snow Resorts Association's site for printable color charts of alpine and nordic codes, as well as illustrated chairlift instructions. Since you're a world traveler, you might want to brush up on the European code, too: *www.fis-ski.com/uk /rulesandpublications/fisgeneralrules/10fisrules.html.%20*.

OUCH!

www.ski-injury.com

Accidents happen, and British physician Mike Langran has some choice photos of displaced wrist fractures to prove it. His detailed guide to the most common skiing and boarding injuries includes statistics from medical studies, causes of injuries, and prevention strategies. Visit the Fit to Ski section for pre-ski warm-up exercises.

15 ALPINE AND TELEMARK SKIING

CORE BEFORE
www.ifyouski.com

You'll look better, feel better, and last longer on the slopes if you get in shape before ski and snowboard season. If You Ski offers free exercise tips recommended by British physiotherapists. Start with some squats and lunges, and then move on to the core training exercises. You can also watch video clips of carving, moguls, steeps, and freeride techniques and read photo-illustrated instructions on snowboard tricks. Scout out European slopes via live webcam, read worldwide snow reports and avalanche information, and book your St. Moritz vacation now. If you really want to get away, visit the resort job listings and make your trip more permanent.

POWDER ALERT
www.snocountry.com

Go straight to the source of all powder news: Snocountry. Get ski reports and snow conditions for your favorite North American resorts and beyond. Sign up for email or cell phone alerts so you can be ready to pack up and go when the flakes start falling. The site also features snow sports industry news, how-to tips, a directory of ski resorts, and photo-illustrated strengthening exercises. Click to your favorite resort to buy season passes, or search the travel section for ski packages.

WHITE ON WHITE
www.couloirmag.com

For skiers and boarders who "earn their turns," and for the rest of us who enjoy watching from the sidelines, *Couloir* magazine's online home is the coolest place to read about backcountry fun (and danger). Check the archives for telemark techniques, a report from the first U.S. randonnée rally, and a gear tester's account of being buried under several feet of snow to test avalanche gear. As you might expect, there are lots of weather and avalanche safety links; there's also a well-attended forum and, my favorite page, an illustrated skiing/boarding glossary.

SKI BETTER
www.skismarts.com

Ski better with Ski Smarts. Determine your level (beginner, intermediate, expert, extreme) using the Lessons Wizard, then follow a series of goal-oriented downhill drills and lessons. Check the Common Problems chart for specific tips and techniques. The professional ski instructors who write the site do an excellent job of posting just the necessary information, nothing extra. They'll tell you why it's important to warm up, clean your skis, and practice exercises and ski skills. If you don't find the answers on the site, email them for a free online ski lesson. Cool.

GLISSE TODAY
www.offpistemag.com

At *Off-Piste* magazine's website, some of the feature stories are a few years old, but the powder's always fresh. Prepare for your backcountry adventure with archived articles on frostbite, shoulder dislocations, acute mountain sickness, and water purification. The Avy 101 section is always relevant, with advice on avalanche courses, beacon technology, and route planning basics. Click on Snow Beta for links to regional weather and avalanche reports, an explanation of avalanche danger codes, safety courses, and recommended reading. Don't miss the photo gallery, technique tips, gear reviews, photo galleries, and a Take Action page with links to backcountry access sites. For the latest features and gear reviews, order the print version.

ASK LOU
www.wildsnow.com

Mountaineer, backcountry skier, and outdoor writer Lou Dawson was the first person to ski all fifty-four of Colorado's 14,000-foot peaks. His backcountry tips cover the importance of duct tape, how to modify a randonnée boot, and the benefits of rechargeable batteries. Visit Dawson's blog for ski trip reports, backcountry news, and his online museum of randonnée bindings. Other blog categories include rando racing, gear reviews, and 8000-meter skiing. There's also a FAQs page with photo examples of how to mount ski bindings.

MAKE TRACKS
www.firsttracksonline.com

Never mind the extra exclamation points, First Tracks!! Online has just the right amount of news, travel, and weather. Find out who just signed with Burton Snowboards, which ski resorts are adding new lifts, and how the U.S. women's ski team training is going. In-depth and inspiring destination features will make it hard to pick your next ski vacation....Utah, Canada, or New Zealand? Thousands read the Liftlines forum for reader-submitted "no bull" snow reports. Extras include nearly three thousand links to sites on snowcat skiing, snowboarding, snowshoeing, resorts, and other snow sports topics.

SHREDDING BETTY
www.alisongannett.com

World freeskiing champion Alison Gannett trekked through all sorts of extreme conditions for seven days to make first tracks on a sacred mountain in Bhutan. Then she went back to the straw-bale home she designed and built in Colorado to plan her next consciousness-raising promotional tour. Read about her skiing and mountain biking adventures, and learn a little bit about solar tax credits and energy efficient home tips.

16 SNOWBOARDING

GOOFY OR REGULAR?
http://users.pandora.be/boarderplanet

Are you goofy or regular? If you don't know the answer, click on Beginner. If you're already shredding, click ahead to the 180, 360, Jump, and Ollie instructions. Boarder Planet has colorful, organized, easy-to-read snowboard lessons for beginners and freestylers. It's not a huge site, and not all descriptions include illustrations or photos, but it's a good place to start. Plus free photos, wallpaper, music downloads, and links to other European boarding sites.

WHAT'S YOUR ANGLE?
www.cs.uu.nl/~daan/snow/stance.html

If you want to get all technical, and I think you should, visit computer programmer and snowboard enthusiast Daan Leijen's site, where you'll find diagrams and charts explaining the crucial whys and hows behind snowboard stances.

ON THE BOARDS
www.boarderline.com

Head for the Boarderline when you're ready to buy a board. Review articles on selecting and caring for your board, and watch demonstration video clips on waxing, using pocket tools, and selecting goggles. If you want to know what to look for when buying a *used* board, how to mount bindings, and how to repair scratches on your board, visit Snowboard City (*www.snowboard-city.com*). They have video clips of stances, grabs, halfpipes, and other tricks. Both are humble little sites and not much to look at, but worth a visit.

FUN AND FRESH
www.bomberonline.com

Shredders will love Bomber Online's boarding articles such as "Your Butt and Where It Should Not Be," "Craving the Carve," and "The Rise and Fall of the Holy Asymmetric Empire." Visit Bomber's Carving Community, a massive online forum where boarders share powder stories, report on resort conditions, comment on races, exchange training tips, sell gear, look for winter condos, and discuss everything else related to hard boots and alpine snowboarding. The site also has a great beginners guide, photo and video galleries, and reader-submitted product reviews. Okay, so I didn't know that Bomber made snowboard bindings until I spent some time on their site, but that's good, right? The site's there for so much more than just shopping.

BOARDING FOR BOOMERS
www.boomerboarding.com/index.shtml

So you're not twenty-five anymore, or even thirty-five. Would you rather sit in your La-Z-Boy eating your shredded wheat, or get out and shred with the best of them? Boomer Boarding is an excellent place to get started, with articles such as "Life on the Edge," "Turn, Turn, Turn," and "Body Parts That Need Protecting." Your host, Gary, aka "Old Rider," will lead you through the basics and tell you what to wear. He also advises on what to look for in a winter resort, reports on resorts he's visited in Colorado, Utah, and New Mexico, and recommends a few pre-season strengthening exercises. From the links page, click to Shred Geezers (*www.shredgeezers.com*), a San Francisco-based boarding club, for some additional inspiration.

SENIOR SHREDDERS
www.graysontrays.com

You don't have to miss out on the fun just because you don't like loud, jargon-filled snowboarding sites produced by twenty-year-olds. Leave the logos and beer bongs behind, and pull up a seat at the adult table. Grays on Trays is one of the best introductions to snowboarding on the web—regardless of your age. Created by a "middle-aged guy from the Midwest," it's humorous, well written, and inspiring (not in a corny way, but in a "get off your bum and try something new" sort of way). You'll need to learn a few basic terms so you can communicate with other boarders, but many, such as "face plant," "butt plant," and "boot" are fairly self-explanatory.

BEGINNING BOARDERS

If you've never been on a snowboard before, **Winter Cream** *(http://users.myexcel.com/wintercream)* can help you lace up, strap up, and find your balance. They'll tell you about some basic turns, how to stop, what to wear, how to fall, and how to select boots and a board.

Next, pay a visit to **Snowboard Essentials** *(www.snowboarding -essentials.com)* to learn the lingo and read up on turns, helmet advice, and tricks and maneuvers you can work up to with practice. The articles don't include demonstration photos or illustrations, however, so click over to **Robert's Ski Instruction** *(www.robertsski.com/webpgss/ski.htm)* for a photo-illustrated mini-lesson.

Finally, at the snowboarding section of **Life Tips** *(http:// snowboard.lifetips.com)*, find bite-size tips on safety, selecting gear and accessories, and tuning your ride.

TRICKS ARE FOR KIDS

www.methodmag.com

If seeing the words "stoked" and "hot chicks" on a website's home page makes you think you're in the wrong place, maybe you are. Or maybe you can get past that. Maybe you just want to follow the Swedish snowboarding team's adventures, check out "Big Moves and Gut-Wrenching Crashes" at the latest challenge, or stay up-to-date on new boards. You can do that at Method, a European snowboard webzine. Rate and share music, download vodcasts of worldwide snowboarding events, and read blogs about the boarding life.

If you and your shreddies are into winter break, coed hot tubbing, snow cams, and boarding videos, you'll probably also love *Snowboarder* magazine's webpage *(www.snowboardermag.com)*. This site has a well-attended forum where the largest discussions are Tech Talk, Industry News, and Style Counsel. Snowboard *(www.snowboard-mag.com)* has a lot of the same, plus online polls about which event has the best teaser and who is the GOAT (greatest of all time).

OLLIE, OLLIE, ALL COME FREE

www.transworldsnowboarding.com

The features read more like blogs, there's an event series with the words "Hot Dawgz" in its title, and a review for a pocket can opener with a special tool for shotgunning. Clearly, it's about youth here. But I still like the Transworld Snowboarding site because there's so much to see: more than one hundred video demonstrations of super cool tricks like kick flips, switch nose presses, and backside sevens; and nearly three hundred videos and teasers from snowboard teams, production companies, resorts, and event producers. I didn't browse them all, but those I checked out were loud and exhilarating. Dude, where's my snowboard?

GIRL POWDER

www.powderroom.net

Read about cat boarding in British Columbia, get the scoop on summer boarding camps, and see what the off-piste situation is at your favorite resort. Get acquainted with the best shredding betties in the business, take a virtual snowboard lesson, and learn how to wax your board. There's also a well-attended forum if you want gossip (their biggest forum category), advice on gear, a ride to the mountain, or trip reports.

17 SNOWSHOEING

STEPPING OUT
www.esnowshoes.com
Find your inner snowshoer at eSnowshoes. The site looks like an online
retailer, but it's actually a great place to learn more about selecting
snowshoes (size does matter), packing your day pack, dressing for success,
and planning snowshoe outings. Of course, there are plenty of click-
through shopping opportunities, but the enthusiasts behind this site
spread the wealth among several online retailers, including Moosejaw,
REI, and Altrec. There's also a guide to snowshoe brands.

DECKED OUT FOR WINTER
www.snowshoemag.com
The folks behind *Snowshoe* magazine want to get people off their couches
and onto snowshoes. A First-Timers Guide will entice you to consider
the sport, and an archive of articles and columns will keep you hooked.
Topics include safety; history (check out the piece on the snowshoe
collection at Yale's Peabody Museum); advice on training, nutrition, and
avoiding snowmobiles; reports on snowshoeing destinations and events;
and product reviews. One of the best features of this site is the searchable
trails database. Find North American snowshoeing clubs and kid-specific
sites in the links section.

SNOWSHOE SCHOOL
www.carlheilman.com/snowshoe.html

Nature photographer, magazine writer, and snowshoe instructor Carl Heilman offers much more than snowshoeing tips and techniques on his website. In addition to archives of his published articles, he employs several colored charts to explain frame and hinge designs, balance and traction issues, and binding styles. Why? So you can understand the snowshoe design and performance features behind different types of snowshoes. A little dry, but worth reviewing, in part because there aren't many other snowshoe-specific sites and blogs. Thanks, Carl.

IF YOU CAN WALK, YOU CAN SNOWSHOE

Here's a tip: You can always find useful how-to and getting-started tips at snowshoe manufacturers' sites. **Tubbs** *(www.tubbssnowshoes.com)* has an excellent worldwide trails database, searchable by difficulty level, distance, and location. Their resource center covers every topic from what to wear and pack to training and planning advice for hiking, running, and backpacking on snowshoes. **Red Feather**'s *(www.redfeather.com)* Snowshoe 101 article covers the basics, plus several useful technique tips and safety recommendations. **Atlas** *(www.atlassnowshoe.com)* has much of the same, with resort information and links to guides and events.

18 NORDIC SKIING

NORDIC KNOW-HOW
www.xcskiworld.com

Recreational and competitive skiers alike will find useful information at the American Cross Country Skiers site. Learn the difference between a snowplow wedge and a half wedge, how and why to wax skis, and most important, how to get up from a fall. If you're beyond that, skip to the Weekly Workout section and articles on dry-land training on roller skis. The site lists XC events around the world, and has plenty of destination pieces about trails in locations as varied as Ely, Minnesota, and Kirkwood, California. Editorials and opinion pieces cover junior through professional events, personalities, and news. There's a forum, too.

GLIDE AWAY
www.crosscountryskier.com

Even though *Cross Country Skier* posts only some of its print articles online, the magazine's site is still worth a look. The Tracks to Try section lists descriptions and contact information for cross-country ski trails, lodges, and resorts in Canada, Colorado, California, Idaho, Minnesota, Montana, New Hampshire, New York, Vermont, Washington, and other snowy states. Check out Nordic News for industry news, event reports, and regional news. You can also access a small selection of destination articles, training features, personal profiles, next season's equipment preview, and World Cup reports. You'll have to subscribe for access to the trail reports.

GROOMED AND READY
www.xcski.org

There are two ways to look for cross-country ski lodges and resorts. The fast way: go to the Cross Country Ski Areas Association and search by state or Canadian province for detailed listings with weblinks. Or the fun, geeky way: Go to Map Muse *(www.mapmuse.com)*, select Sports and Recreation from a list of interests, then click on Cross-country Skiing. Finally, click on your state of interest. You'll get a map of the area, marked with ski resorts, plus descriptions of lodges, trail information, an area weather report, driving instructions, and links to each resort (which usually take you back to the CCSAA site, where you can find directories for guided tours, travel, and gear manufacturers). Kids will like the animated Snowmonsters section on CCSAA, where they can play video games, learn about nature, and watch snow-sports cartoons.

FIND YOUR MATE
If you break or lose a ski, there's still hope. Check for a match at *www.brokenski.com*.

BIG SKY BLOGGER
www.ernordic.com/ralph.htm

So it's not organized by topic; half the fun at Ralph's Nordic Web blog is clicking on a title to see if an article appears or an entire month of posts. Cleaning and storing skis, marathon waxing (lots of waxing info here), skating techniques, and ski walking are just a few of his topics, most with photos and illustrations. If you're looking for motivation, follow Ralph on moonlight and backcountry ski outings, via his favorite trail reports. During winter months, Ralph also provides Montana ski and weather reports and a directory of regional nordic event listings.

LIVE THE BIRKIE
www.birkie.com

By late February, normal people are going crazy from cabin fever and checking airfares to Mexico. Meanwhile, nordic skiers are flocking to the frigid plains of Wisconsin to ski the Birkie, a 51-kilometer race based on an eight-hundred-year-old Norwegian legend. Planners usually expect around nine thousand skiers and more than fifteen thousand spectators for an American Birkebeiner race. You can catch "Birkie Fever" even if long-distance competition isn't your thing; the weekend event also has fun and competitive ski races for kids and adults, nature hikes, elite sprints, and ski demonstrations.

TRAIL TRAINING
www.nordicskiracer.com

Stay in ski shape year-round with Nordic Ski Racer's training pages. The site features articles on finding your training zone, pre- and post-race fueling, and other competition-related topics. There are also photo-illustrated plyometric drills, strength-training exercises, and core-strengthening moves with a medicine ball. For the off-season, you'll find articles on roller skiing techniques, news reports, and gear reviews. Site host Michigan skier Mike Muha includes his training journal as well as useful information for Michigan skiers, such as weather and snow conditions and forecasts, upcoming events, and links to waxing tips.

THINGS TO DO, PLACES TO GO

Wilderness areas are first of all a series of sanctuaries for the primitive arts of wilderness travel, especially canoeing and packing.

— Aldo Leopold

19 PARKS AND TRAILS

84 MILLION ACRES OF FUN

www.nps.gov

Want to explore coral reef beds off the coast of Florida or lava tube caves in California? Or is rock climbing at Arches National Park more your style? There are more than 300 recreation areas in the national park system. Search the NPS site by state, park name, or activity to find park descriptions, photos, history and cultural information, climate news, trip planning details, and fun facts about park wildlife, history, and geology. As you know, reserving campsites at the most popular parks can be brutally difficult; this site can help you look beyond Yellowstone. Walk among redwoods in South Carolina, soak in mountain hot springs in Washington, or go all Richard Dreyfuss and make the trek to Devils Tower in Wyoming. NPS sells national park passes online, as well as printed national park guides.

VIRTUAL TOURS

http://travel.discovery.com

Although it's a super commercial site—sometimes you even have to watch a short commercial before you get to view the video feature stories, especially if there's a celebrity involved—The Travel Channel is still a top outdoor resource, with breathtaking photos of scenery and wildlife from your favorite national parks, as well as articles, videos, podcasts, gear advice, and 300,000 reader-submitted travel reviews. You're sure to find more activities and destinations here than you could ever fit in your outdoor to-do list. They may do an even better job of describing the national parks than the National Parks Service does, but I guess they have a bigger budget. You can book a trip from the site, or use Quick Links to find vacation packages, travel deals, and more.

OH, THE PLACES YOU'LL GO
www.trails.com

Planning a mountain biking outing in Utah or a kayaking trip in Baja just got very easy. Or maybe you'd rather go backpacking along the Appalachian Trail? Wherever you want to go, you'll be able to find your way at Trails.com, a database of 30,000 North American trails. This site is professional, organized, and easy to use. You can trust the trail descriptions, driving directions, and maps because they come from actual guidebooks—1000 guidebooks to be exact—from a variety of outdoor publishers. Download maps and print out trail descriptions to throw in your day pack. After a free fourteen-day trial membership, you have to become a member for full access to the site, but even with limited access, you can find some useful trail details.

START AT THE SOURCE
www.trailsource.com

Trailsource may not have the gargantuan database that Trails.com does, but it still has thousands of trail listings and maps for hiking, biking, skiing, boarding, horseback riding, and other outdoor pursuits. Each category has its own start page, where you can click on Hot Picks, New Additions, or Quick Links to worldwide destinations. Click anywhere on the world map, and you'll get a detailed map of the region marked with trails. They even have maps of ski runs. Trail descriptions include plenty of photos, lodging information, weblinks, and even hot breakfast spots. The only downside—you need a subscription to view most of the site.

EVERYPLACE WILD
www.wildernet.com

It's wild. It's green. And it's free! Wildernet is the gateway to forty thousand recreational opportunities in the United States. Search by state, activity, or scenery to find national forests, state parks, wildlife refuges, historic sites, guided trips, picnic spots, and scenic drives. This site is so organized and easy to use, you'll want to spend hours researching and planning trips. Find a campsite in Florida or cross-country ski trails in Wisconsin! Destinations are listed in simple chart format, along with quick facts such as location, park fees, degree of difficulty, and reservation information. Click on a destination for brief descriptions, trip reports, and climate conditions. You can reserve some campsites online, and there's a trip planner for booking lodging and transportation. Shop for gear via Wildernet's retail partner, Altrec.com.

THE HISTORY OF TRAILS

www.fs.fed.us/recreation/programs/trails/nat_trails.shtml

Following Lewis and Clark's trail is *so* last year. Instead, why not pretend you're a 19th century gold prospector and travel by dog sled along the Iditarod National Historic Trail? Or retrace the wagon trail route along the Oregon National Historic Trail, with 125 historic sites along the way? The National Trails System, which has hundreds of recreational trails as well as the seventeen historic and scenic trails, should have its own site, but it doesn't. So you'll have to visit the USDA Forest Service site for an overview of the trails system, a downloadable map, and trail descriptions. Then visit the National Park Service website (see 84 Million Acres of Fun, page 97) for more information on specific trails.

STATE TRAILS

www.americantrails.org

American Trails is an excellent source for North American recreational trails. From the Trails page, click on your state or Canadian province of choice for links to trail administrators—generally, the Department of Natural Resources and the National Park Service. The rest of the page contains links that runners, hikers, mountain bikers, cross-country skiers, equestrians, and paddlers can use to locate specific trails, hook up with outdoor clubs, download maps, and connect with at least one state advocacy organization. Click on Official State Park Pages to visit park sites for each state. Another option: click on National Recreation Trails to find a database of more than nine hundred trails, searchable by activity, length, location, state, and facilities.

RECYCLED TRAILS
www.railstrails.org
www.traillink.com
www.trailsfromrails.com

The Rails-to-Trails Conservancy is all about converting retired railway corridors to recreational trails, such as the Fox River Trail in Illinois and Virginia's W&OD Trail. With more than 1300 trails in the TrailLink database, runners, cyclists, walkers, inline skaters, and even equestrians can find a way to get from A to B that doesn't involve a car. Searchable by state, activity, and other variables, thorough trail descriptions cover all the essentials, from trail length, surface, permitted activities, and wheelchair accessibility, to printable maps, trail reviews, and photos. Since many rail trails are in rural areas, you may also want to check out Trails from Rails for related guidebooks and nearby accommodations and attractions.

THE URBAN APPALACHIAN TRAIL
www.greenway.org

Not all thru-hikers want to be in the woods for months. I'd rather walk, bike, or inline skate from city to city, enjoying the green in between. The East Coast Greenway Alliance is working hard to establish a 2950-mile car-free corridor from Maine to Florida. (Imagine cycling to spring break!) Only 21 percent of the route is established so far, so they need your help to complete the route. Even if you don't live on the East Coast, get online, join the cause, and help make it happen.

TRAILKEEPERS
www.wta.org

For an advocacy organization, the Washington Trails Association is a lot of fun. Their photo gallery will make you envious (or maybe not, maybe you've been somewhere even more amazing and have a photo of your own to add), and the hiking guide includes 171 volunteer-written trail descriptions for all sorts of activities in the Northwest, plus essential packing and weather information, a reading list, backcountry cooking recipes, and trail etiquette tips. You can search for trails by distance, location, elevation gain, or other parameters—and submit a report of your own if you have a hike to share. When you're ready to give back, check the action alerts section for current projects: you can join a trail restoration crew for a day (or a week), use the online activist tools to write letters to Congress, or work at the WTA office. Of course, you can always send money.

ON THE ROAD AGAIN
Plan your next road trip at these webside attractions:
   www.roadtripusa.com/jamiesblog.html
   www.roadsideamerica.com
   www.roadtripmemories.com

NATIONAL PARKS NEWS
www.nationalparkstraveler.com
You can spend hours at Kurt Repanshek's well-designed, content-rich National Parks Traveler blog. Read about mountain goats in Glacier National Park, dinosaur tracks on Denali, or a wildflower festival at Cedar Breaks National Monument; look for the best lodging deals at Zion, Shenandoah, Sequoia, and other parks; or stay up-to-date on park management and stewardship issues. There are book and gear reviews, too. The big bonus, though: Parks Connections, which features links to some of the best national park sites out there, like the American Park Network, the National Parks Conservation Association, and the U.S. National Parks and Monuments Travel Guide.

MIND YOUR MANNERS
www.emilypost.com
www.fs.fed.us/r8/boone/safety/camp/share_trail.shtml
Just because you're outdoors doesn't mean you leave your manners at home. You know all about the Leave No Trace principles, and you would never violate park regulations. Still, it can't hurt to review some basic etiquette guidelines before heading into the wilderness. The Emily Post Institute isn't just about tea parties; they'll tell you how to behave on the trail and on the ski slopes, too.

Many hiking organizations, as well as state and national parks, also include trail etiquette for hikers, skiers, cyclists, pet owners, and equestrians on their sites. Forest Service sites (such as *www.fs.fed.us/r8/boone/safety /camp/share_trail.shtml*) are also a great source for trail guidelines.

20 CAMPING

BACKCOUNTRY BASICS
www.wenzelco.com

There's a lot of camping information on the web, but it's usually tucked into a backpacking article or relegated to just a few tips on national park sites. I wanted a stand-alone guide with getting started instructions. I finally found exactly what I needed at the Wenzel tent company's site. Their Camping Info section has great advice for first-time campers. They tell you how to prepare for the trip, what to pack, how to set up camp, what to eat, and what you'll need for the road trip to the campsite, plus many useful tips. For example, did you know an inflated ziplock bag makes an extra pillow in a pinch? If you're camping with kids, there are car and camp games to keep them amused. The Wenzel Company pros even coach you on how to tell a good campfire story. For more backcountry basics, check out the Austrailian site Open Road *(www.openroad.com.au)* for their 40 Great Camping Tips.

LOVING THE OUTDOORS
www.lovetheoutdoors.com

It's not the fanciest site, but Love the Outdoors has everything you need to get out there and start lovin'. Links to private, state, and national parks help you blaze a trail to the campsites you want. Use their packing and first-aid lists to make sure you have all the gear you need. Browse the skills area to learn how to build a campfire, how to keep bugs at bay, how to practice the Leave No Trace principles, what to wear, and more. There are also sections on cooking, camp songs and stories, a photo gallery, and links to camping organizations. Camp Necessities *(www.campnecessities .com)* is another resource for food checklists, recipes, and camping tips.

TERROR TALES
www.halloween-website.com/tales.htm

Why even have a campfire if you're not going to scare the crap out of the kids with stories about ax murderers and crazy ghost ladies? Or at least get them to jump every time a twig snaps. Halloween Web ("Where things go bump in the night") is a good place to stock up on the spooky stuff. You'll find classic urban legends such as "The Hook," "The Killer in the Backseat," and "Tap, Tap, Tap." Those always work well. Also check American Folklore *(www.americanfolklore.net)* for tales of ghostly ghouls, menacing monsters, and spine-chilling spirits.

21 ECO TRAVEL

ECO ESCAPES
www.ecotourism.org

Before you book your vacation at that so-called eco resort in the Caribbean, you might want to learn the eco rules. Any hotel can add "eco" to its name, but hotels and resorts listed in the International Ecotourism Society database have to sign a code of conduct to earn their eco status. You'll find a definition of ecotourism here, as well as a searchable list of travel agents, accommodations, and travel services committed to eco principles. Sustainable Travel International *(www.sustainabletravelinternational.org)* is another site you can use for eco travel planning. Download information on responsible travel, learn about carbon offsets, and search the directory for vacation packages and tour operators.

WILL WORK FOR ORGANIC FOOD
www.coralcay.org
www.wwoofhawaii.org

So you can't afford the fancy paradise eco lodge with handmade soaps and exotic organic fruit plates—you can still take a scuba diving vacation in Fiji. Join a Coral Cay Conservation Expedition in Fiji, Tobago, or the Philippines, and spend your days exploring and studying coral reefs. If it's the fruit you're after, you can harvest pineapple and mangoes on an organic farm in Hawaii. You won't get six-hundred-thread-count sheets on your volunteer vacation, but you'll be comfortable enough in your yurt or tent.

WANTED: RESEARCH ASSISTANTS
www.earthwatch.org

You could go home for the holidays, or you could study monkeys in Costa Rica. The Earthwatch Institute offers more than 140 expeditions around the world. Search their site by location or date, and find scientific expeditions that need your help. Walk with the rhinos, swim with the sharks, or watch the birds and the bees do the pollination thing in prairie meadows. Once you read the expedition blogs and field journals, you'll want to go. Check the events section to find an Earthwatch lecture or special event in your city.

CLEAN AND GREEN
www.greenhotels.com

Sure, you're all green and conscientious, but how do you keep it up on the road? You can start by asking your hotel *not* to change your sheets and towels every day. If you're staying at a "green" hotel, they probably already have request cards for that purpose. The Green Hotels Association's site features many such green lodgings committed to energy-saving and waste-reducing housekeeping practices. Participating businesses range from bed-and-breakfast inns, to popular chain hotels such as Howard Johnson, EconoLodge, and Holiday Inn, to the more upscale Hilton. The site also provides "green" tips for travelers and money-saving suggestions for hotel managers who want to reduce their venue's environmental impact. For a more extensive database of hotels, motels, and resorts with green ratings and details on green practices, also visit the Best Green Hotels section of Environmentally Friendly Hotels *(www.environmentallyfriendlyhotels.com)*.

BE A LOW-IMPACT TRAVELER
www.terrapass.com

You recycle. You ride your bike to work. You've got a worm bin. But how can you be a low-impact traveler when your next big adventure is a ten-hour drive or a five-hour flight away? You buy a TerraPass to offset the amount of pollution your journey creates. Then the folks at TerraPass invest the money in renewable energy projects. Check out their blog for green living tips and information on global warming. For another viewpoint on carbon trading, visit Britain's Climate Care *(www.climatecare.org)*.

22 ADVENTURE RACING

"IT'S A KILLER"
www.canadiandeathrace.com

Running marathons and climbing mountains just aren't enough for some people. They have to do more. They have to run the Canadian Death Race, a 125-kilometer wilderness course that involves crossing a river, summiting three mountains, and gaining seventeen thousand feet in elevation. Personally, I'd rather eat my hiking boots, but if it sounds like a happy jaunt to you, check it out. And while you're out there trying to kill yourself, the race organizers have thoughtfully arranged fun for the whole family and friends at the related Adventure Festival.

AN URBAN JUNGLE
www.urbanadventureracing.com/scallion

Not all adventures happen in the wild. There's an urban jungle out there to be explored. So get your team together, and suit up. Chicago's Wild Scallion, part of the Wild Onion Urban Adventure Race series, is an all-day endurance event involving scooters, skating, cycling, running, orienteering, stair climbing, and an undisclosed water event. You can find a team and training programs on the Scallion site. The main Onion site *(www .urbanadventureracing.com/wildonion.html)* hasn't been updated for a few years, but it is still a useful source of training and competition articles.

HOT, HOT, HOT
www.sierraadventuresports.com

Get all hot under the collar playing outdoor games with Sierra Adventure Sports. Check their site for multi-event adventure races in the Southwest. Run, orienteer, paddle, cycle, hike, tube, and trek through urban courses or natural wonders. Go solo, compete with a team, or volunteer on race day. SAS also produces several women-only events.

SIX DEGREES OF NAVIGATION
www.cascadeoc.org/Degrees/SixHome.html

I like an event that's not just about skill and athletic prowess, but that requires some serious geek power. In the Six Degrees of Navigation adventure race, you can't win if you can't use a compass. Navigate your way to sprints in mountain biking, trekking, kayaking, and other events. There's also a kayak-free race category for those who prefer to stay on terra firma. The Cascade Orienteering Club in Washington State sponsors this low-key event. Check with your local orienteering club for similar events.

YOU COULD BE OUTSIDE 24/7
Find more adventure races at *www.sleepmonsters.us*.

GO GREENLAND
www.atc.gl

What do you do when you've done it all? You go to Greenland and spend four days trekking over glaciers and mountains, paddling through ice fjords, and riding a mountain bike along roads and rivers, wherever they may wind. Sound like a good time? Sign up fast because the Arctic Team Challenge only accepts fifteen teams of four. If you want to see what you're in for, or what you're going to miss, watch the race's promotional video. Then click to the East Greenland tourism site for slideshows of the terrain and information on recreational opportunities and local history.

BUST A GUT
www.raidthenorth.com

When race organizers refer to the finish line as "a very small part of the Raid the North experience," it's pretty obvious that this 36-hour adventure race through the Canadian backcountry is more than a little hard-core. But it's good to know you get props for trying. Here's how it works: four-person coed teams trek 30–60 kilometers, ride mountain bikes 60–100 kilometers, and paddle and portage 20 or 30 kilometers. Oh, yeah, and there's a ropes section in there somewhere. If this doesn't sound tough enough, click through to Raid the North Extreme—you'll be on the move nonstop for six days. (FYI, search and rescue teams are standing by.)

COLD PLAY
www.rockandiceultra.com

What is it about these Canadians and all their extreme races? The Rock and Ice Ultra is yet another wilderness challenge in which participants race against time, weather, and unforgiving terrain. This time, individuals run, snowshoe, and ski their way through the Canadian desert (otherwise known as the subarctic Northwest Territories), where race temperatures average between –23° and –11°C. The Ultra offers four events: a 5K fun run, a fifty-mile race over frozen lakes and trails, a hundred-mile race over several frozen lakes and land portages, and a six-stage 186-mile foot and snowshoe race through the wilderness (in which you have to carry your own food, pack, and sleeping bag). Do you really have that much to prove? If you do, then check the site for registration information as well as gear and racing tips.

WILDLIFE

It is not so much for its beauty that the forest makes a claim upon men's hearts, as for that subtle something, that quality of air, that emanation from old trees, that so wonderfully changes and renews a weary spirit.
— Robert Louis Stevenson

23 FLORA AND FAUNA

THE HILLS ARE ALIVE

www.wildflowerinformation.org

It's a treat to find a new wildflower, which is why you should always take a camera on your hikes. When you get home, visit the American Meadows Wildflower Information Lookup site to identify the flower(s) you discover. Search by color, height, location, or half a dozen other variables. Stick around to find out how the forget-me-not got its name and how Native Americans used a medicinal plant named turtlehead to treat skin disorders. The Lady Bird Johnson Wildflower Center *(www .wildflower.org)* is another excellent resource, with a database of 7175 species, more than 19,000 photo images, and links to wildflower and native plant societies across the country. Both sites contain growing information and sell seeds.

NATURAL TREASURES

www.pbs.org/americanfieldguide/

You only have so much vacation time, so when you need a nature fix, visit American Field Guide. Produced by Oregon Public Broadcasting, this easy-to-navigate site has 1400 video clips that let you get all up-close and personal with carnivorous beetles in Texas; pelicans, coots, and grackles in Louisiana's Sabine Wildlife Refuge; and Red Hill salamanders in Alabama. Watch short programs on tide pools, grasslands, deserts, and canyon ecosystems. Learn about fossils, plants, glaciers, search and rescue dogs, restoring river otter populations, and maintaining national parks. Why read when you can watch?

WILD KINGDOM

http://animal.discovery.com

Headline news: "Beetles Seduce Bees to Survive." Read all about it, watch the video, and get all interactive at the Discovery Channel's *Animal Planet* series website. Hang around and play the Meercat Manor Maze game, get a sneak peak of the cable series' upcoming shows, and if you have the bandwidth, definitely tune in to *Mutual of Omaha's Wild Kingdom* (it's all new), where you can watch clips of sea snakes, cobras, anteaters, and Tasmanian devils. Or, if you're on the go, just download the podcast. Don't miss the Steve "Croc Hunter" Irwin memorial page.

WHOSE SCAT IS THAT?

You're not alone out there. Wild turkeys, skunks, porcupines, and other critters could be stalking you at every step. Take the free tracks and scat quizzes at **North Woods Guides** *(www.northwoodsguides.com)* to learn who's been on the trail before you got there...and might still be lurking nearby. Learn more about your little friends, and about black bears, bobcats, coyotes, and moose, in the Field Notes section.

Protrails *(http://protrails.com)* also offers basic information about animal tracks. Click on a track for descriptions and photos of the mountain lion, the Collared Peccary, and the yellow-bellied marmot. For tracking techniques and activities, color scat photos, and an impressive collection of track illustrations and explanations, visit Beartracker's Animal Tracks Den *(www.bear-tracker.com)*. Finally, just because it's cold outdoors doesn't mean all the animals are hibernating. Visit **Andy's Northern Ontario Wildflower** site *(www.ontariowildflower.com)* for winter tracks photos.

ANIMALS ONLINE

www.nationalgeographic.com

Raccoons have the cutest cousins! They're called kukajous, and they live in trees in Central and South America. Kukajous love fruit, and they can run in any direction. That's just a speck of what you can learn at National Geographic. There are photos, audio files, and articles on every type of animal and bug, and news stories on global warming, archeology, and history. They'll even tell you how to take better photos. You can watch a video of a sewer diver, read about cat-murdering raccoons (not to be mistaken for kukajous; kukajous are nonviolent and basically vegans), email friends an article about making ethanol out of cow manure (don't try this at home), and print all sorts of maps. If you're on the go, download news stories, interviews with scientists and explorers, and audio tours of the best urban and wilderness walks and treks to your iPod for free. Click to the National Geographic Channel site for more videos and program previews.

STAYING ALIVE

> *Getting to the summit is optional. Getting back down is mandatory.*
>
> — Ed Viesturs

24 GO WITH GUIDES

PEAK TO PEAK
www.rmiguides.com
Cofounded by world-renowned mountaineer Lou Whittaker, Rainier Mountaineering has been leading climbers to the highest peaks since 1969. They offer guiding services for Mount Rainier and Mount McKinley, and lead climbing trips in Ecuador, Argentina, Africa, Russia, and Europe. Their team of expert guides includes world-class climber Ed Viesturs. Check out their photo galleries for inspiration, then click to the training section for your pre-climb prep.

DREAM FLOWS
www.aorafting.com
For the same reasons you wouldn't climb a 14,000-foot peak by yourself, it's probably not a good idea to just jump in a raft and hope for the best. All Outdoors has been guiding paddlers through white water since 1962. They offer beginning through class 5 level paddles on ten California rivers. Their site contains packing lists, directions, accommodations, and everything else you need to know before your trip.

RED ROCKS WEST
www.moabdesertadventures.com
For your next desert adventure, explore slot canyons, climb sandstone towers, and rappel from arches. Moab Desert Adventures is the longest running climbing guide service in Moab, and all of its guides have completed American Mountain Guides Association training. MDA also leads

a climbing trip in Nevada and organizes Chicks on Crags, a women's climbing event. For more information on canyoneering, visit Canyoneering USA *(www.canyoneeringusa.com)* and The American Canyoneering Association *(www.canyoneering.net)*.

ICE AND SNOW

www.cougarmountain.ca
www.skithetetons.com
www.ourayclimbing.com

It's much more relaxing to snowshoe through the backcountry when you're not worried about dying in an avalanche or getting lost and turning blue with hypothermia. Not that having a guide guarantees your safety—but it increases your odds. Cougar Mountain Adventures offers two- to three-hour walks in British Columbia's Whistler backcountry. If you're looking for a longer outing, Rendezvous Backcountry Tours of Ski the Tetons leads guided hut-to-hut skiing, boarding, and snowshoeing trips. Learn how to ice climb, or book a customized ice adventure with San Juan Mountain Guides, headquartered in Ouray, Colorado. (They also lead expeditions and climbing trips in Colorado, Europe, and South America.)

25 SURVIVAL AND SAFETY SKILLS

ONLY YOU
www.smokeybear.com

Smokey Bear is still around, and now he has his own website. Pay the old bruin a visit and ramble through a virtual museum of Smokey posters through the decades. It's still up to you to prevent forest fires, though, so you'll also want to review the fire safety tips. Stick around for information on good fires and bad fires, the science of fires, and a look at how smoke-jumpers and land crews fight wildfires.

For more in-depth articles and statistics, Smokey provides links to NOVA's wildfire simulator, other fire safety websites, the Forest History Society, and Yellowstone's fire ecology reports. The kids section has video games, Smokey's profile, and a fill-in-the-blanks storyteller. Extras include a downloadable curricula guide for teachers.

SURVIVAL LIGHT
www.bcadventure.com

For basic wilderness safety and survival tips, BCAdventure, a Canadian tourism site, is a good place to start. They cover essential skills such as measuring distance; navigating across land using a compass, the stars, and the sun; building a fire; and making an emergency shelter. Their first-aid guide includes instructions for treating a variety of hot and cold weather ailments, including shock, sprains, burns, bites, and snow blindness.

SURVIVAL ENCYCLOPEDIA
www.surviveoutdoors.com

Survive Outdoors covers just about every wilderness peril from heat stroke to hypothermia to lightning exposure, plus stings, bites, fevers, viruses, and bubonic plague. In case you need any safety reminders, there are cautionary photos of sea lice bites, dislocated joints, and fishhook-impaled forearms. Not to worry, though, the doctors behind this site provide introductory information, dispel myths, describe symptoms, and detail recommended medical treatment for each health concern. As an added bonus, get a lesson in distinguishing between dangerous spiders and snakes and the merely creepy crawlers.

ITCHY BUSINESS
www.americanhiking.org

Bugs suck, and then you get West Nile virus. Of course, it probably won't happen to you, but it couldn't hurt to read the bugs fact sheet at the American Hiking Society website. While you're there, read the snake fact sheet, the sun fact sheet, and anything else you think might help you make it home alive and well. Still worried about West Nile? Or have you moved on to Lyme disease? Better check Medline *(www.nlm.nih.gov /medlineplus)*, too, to see what the professionals say.

AUTO ADAPTATION
You never know when you might get lost, dumped, or fired. Or decide to take a year off to explore national parks across the country. Learn to live in your car at *www.carliving.net*.

ARE YOU A SURVIVOR?
www.wilderness-survival.net

How long could you survive in the wilderness? Take Sergeant Safari's Survival Quiz to find out. Wilderness Survival's skills pages are based on a U.S. Army survival guide, and cover twenty-two major skills areas for jungle, forest, desert, and open water survival. There are illustrated guides to building fires, making distress signals, crossing rivers, and other core techniques. Plus, reference guides on dangerous snakes and edible plants, and packing lists for survival kits. Wilderness Manuals *(www.wildernessmanuals.com)* has similar army-based advice, including navigation skills, trail first aid, and field hygiene and safety.

SAFETY SCHOOL
www.princeton.edu/~oa/resources

Princeton University's Outdoor Action Guides can be a bit dry, but they're always streamlined and organized. These folks know how to prepare for river trips, design safety plans, and deal with environmental and physical hazards. Read the OA Guides to Outdoor Safety Management, Developing a Safety Management Program, and Running a Safe River Trip to learn why common accidents occur and how to prevent them. Don't miss the paddling decision tree, an essential tool for group outings. You can test your knowledge with kayaking and hiking accident scenarios—but only Princeton students can access the answers. (Survival of the fittest?!)

BE BEAR AWARE
www.bearsmart.com

Don't ruin a stellar hike or camping trip by getting mauled by a bear. The Get Bear Smart Society has you covered, with articles, tips, and guidelines about hiking and camping in bear country. Learn the difference between black bears and grizzly bears, how to store and dispose of food and garbage, and what to do in a bear encounter. If you're still nervous, there are several brochures you can download for more information —"Recreating in Bear, Wolf, and Mountain Lion Country" was my favorite. The GBSS also leads bear-viewing trips in Canada, Alaska, and Minnesota.

THE CAT OF ONE COLOR
www.mountainlion.org

Mountain lion. Cougar. Puma. They're all the same. These big cats rarely attack humans—they're more interested in eating your pets and livestock—but you should still be prepared. The Mountain Lion Foundation has twelve safety tips for living and hiking in cougar country. Maybe if you learn more about them, you'll learn to love them and join the fight to protect them. Get more cougar information and safety tips at the Cougar Fund *(www.cougarfund.org)*.

PRESCRIPTION: PERIL
www.doctordanger.com

Sure, it's all fun and games until someone loses an eye. Is it worth it for a chance to ride a street luge down a mountain road at 80 mph, run with the bulls in Pamplona, or roll cheese down steep hills in Gloucestershire? Probably. But as the guys at Doctor Danger say, "Remember: 'Shit Happens.' If you go mountain biking, sooner or later you will crash." So you might as well prepare yourself and hope for the best. Learn how to select a bike helmet, how to survive a surfing wipe out, how to not become shark bait, and what to do if a bull gores you. They'll even tell you how to donate your organs...just in case you perish in a cheese rolling competition.

LIFE PRESERVERS
www.riveroflifefarm.com/hiking/hiking-safety-rules.html

Could there be a more auspicious place for hiking safety information than along the banks of the River of Life? Ozarks wilderness outfitters Myron and Ann McKee provide excellent commonsense safety tips on their site for hiking in the Mark Twain National Forest, or in any forest. They also provide a link to online retailer Altrec.com's backcountry skills page *(www.altrec.com/published/camp/skills/backcountryhikingsafety/)*. I like the Danger/Remedy format Altrec uses to remind readers that preparation is key.

26 WILDERNESS AND LEADERSHIP TRAINING

TAKE THE LEAD
www.nols.edu

Wouldn't it be nice to really know what you're doing when you head off on a kayaking or hiking expedition? The respected National Outdoor Leadership School (NOLS) offers leadership training courses in just about every outdoor activity, including backpacking, camping, climbing, paddling, skiing, boarding, and wilderness medicine. With courses for teenagers, including semester abroad programs such as kayaking in New Zealand for college credit, the NOLS programs may seem geared toward a younger crowd, but they also offer adult education courses. Trained instructors teach all courses, with an emphasis on mastering outdoor skills and developing leadership qualities. Graduates of their thirty-day programs are qualified to lead group wilderness trips. Author and war correspondent Sebastian Junger and climber and filmmaker David Breashears are both NOLS alums.

BE ALL YOU CAN BE
www.outwardboundwilderness.org

Find yourself; develop your character. That's what Outward Bound is all about. They offer outdoor educational programs for children and at-risk youth, team-building courses for professionals, and wilderness adventures for explorers of all ages. Learn dog sledding in Minnesota, sailing in Florida, or desert backpacking in Texas. Course lengths range from a few days to a few months.

MOUNTAIN MATTERS
www.outdoors.org/education

If you can't take off a month to become a kayak guide, how about spending a day or a weekend learning backpacking basics, how to rock climb, or how to take nature photos? The Appalachian Mountain Club, with several chapters in the Northeast, offers outdoor skills and naturists workshops, school and family programs, and summer camps, as well as outreach courses for at-risk youth. If you want to be really useful, they also offer wilderness first-responder and first-aid certification courses. Courses are listed on the site; check AMC chapter sites for more programs.

WILDERNESS TRACKING
www.trackerschool.com

Developing wilderness skills can save your life; communing with the spirits of Apache scouts can change your soul. Tom Brown Jr.'s Tracking and Survival School in New Jersey offers seventy-five wilderness classes in eight study tracks—all based on Native American philosophies and techniques. Students learn nature observation and tracking, primitive tool making, water collection, trapping, and other essential skills, while developing greater awareness of their surroundings. Brown, who learned at the feet of an Apache elder, has been leading courses for thirty years. (Also see Peter Wolf's Tracking and Wilderness Skills training programs, which include instruction in urban disasters survival, at *www.wolfskills.com*.)

KEEP IT SIMPLE
www.boss-inc.com

Low tech, high experience. That's what the Utah-based Boulder Outdoor Survival School (BOSS) promises. They'll send you into the desert with only a knife, a poncho, and a blanket, and see how you do. BOSS offers 7-, 14-, and 28-day field courses, wilderness medical certification, and less intense skills and explorer courses in desert and alpine terrains. Before you go, read up on flint knapping and buck skinning at The History and Primitive Technology Page *(www.onagocag.com)*.

CLIMB EVERY MOUNTAIN

www.mtnguide.com

You've heard the call of the wild, and it's telling you to climb a mountain. The American Alpine Institute offers group and individual instruction in essential alpine skills, including rescue and medical training, and leads treks and expeditions around the world. They have courses for climbers of all experience levels, as well as women-only programs. Learn desert rock climbing in Nevada, ice climbing in Washington, and leadership skills in California. When you're ready for some serious altitude training, there are AAI trips to Bolivia and China.

27 WEATHER

PARTLY SUNNY, WITH A CHANCE OF FUN
www.weather.com

I used to make fun of people who watched the Weather Channel, but I take it all back after using their website. The Weather Channel online has it all. Say you want to surf in Southern California—with a few clicks, you can check tides, wave height, and wind speed at your favorite beaches. Maybe you're planning a backpacking trip in Colorado; check daily, hourly, and extended weather forecasts, plus sun and moon times, pollen count, and mosquito activity for state and national parks. There's more than weather here; the site also provides descriptions of outdoor destinations, safety tips, and mini activity guides. If you really want to get all geeky about it, there are webcams, downloadable radar maps, and email storm alerts too. Stay informed on the road or trail with free customized wireless phone weather reports. For similar content, see Wunderground *(www .wunderground.com),* Accuweather *(www.accuweather.com)*, and Intellicast *(www.intellicast.com).*

FOLLOW THE JETSTREAM
www.nws.noaa.gov
www.noaa.gov

You'll want to spend hours at the National Oceanic and Atmospheric Administration (NOAA) site. Start with the National Weather Service for nationwide weather forecasts, storm predictions and warnings, climate outlooks, air quality reports, and historical weather data. Then visit the NOAA home page for links to nautical charts; tide and current information; aviation-related weather forecasts; and to "hot topics" such as floods, earthquakes, El Niño, and volcanoes. The coolest part of the site is Jetstream, an online weather guide where you can learn about the ocean, different types of thunderstorms, lightning safety, and remote sensing. There are even review quizzes at the end of each chapter. To further your weather education, visit The Weather World Report 2010 Project *(http://ww2010.atmos.uiuc.edu/(Gh)/home.rxml)*.

WEATHER WHIRL
www.wildwildweather.com
http://weatherpixie.com

Listen to the sounds of rain, a hurricane, and a tornado at Dan's Wild Wild Weather Page. Designed for kids but also ideal for adults, this fun site makes it easy to learn why it rains, how wind is created, and what makes hurricanes happen. Weatherman Dan's illustrated explanations are easy to follow, and he provides several links to learning activities you can do at home, such as "how to track a hurricane," "how to create a tornado," and "measuring the sound of thunder." If you'd like to report the weather on your own website, visit Weather Pixie to create a pixie icon, which updates your readers as the weather changes.

GROUND CONTROL TO MAJOR TOM
www.spaceweather.com

So it's snowing in Denver or there's a lightning storm in Minneapolis—what about the weather in space? Might be a good idea to check out geomagnetic storms, track asteroids, view coronal holes, and review solar flare forecasts before you leave the house. Click on Aurora Mega Gallery to view photos of "northern lights" (aka aurora borealis) from around the world. Follow the many sun links to hot sites on comets, sunspots, sun dogs, rainbows, and solar-terrestrial physics.

OUTDOOR COMMUNITY

One touch of nature makes the whole world kin.
— William Shakespeare

28 FRIENDS... AND MAYBE MORE?

THE MORE, THE MERRIER

www.naturistsociety.com

One club does not fit all, but you can be sure that there are plenty of like-minded souls out there, no matter what your outdoor interest. Maybe you want to find women-only hiking outings, or meet other BMW motorcycle owners who camp, or join a nudist (sorry, "naturist") paddling club. No problem. Wander Women *(www.wander-women.com)* is a women's hiking club in Arizona; from the photos on their site, it looks like they have a lot of fun. The Madison BMW Club organizes ride and camp events *(www.madisonbmwclub.org)*. If you're looking for clothing-free fun in the outdoors, you have several options, including the Naturist-Christian Organization *(www.naturist-christians.org)* and the Naturist Society *(www.naturistsociety.com)*, which also has a singles interest group *(www.sunclad.com/singles)*. If none of these groups sound like your cup of tea, Peak to Peak *(www.peaktopeak.net)* and Johann and Sandra's Web *(www.johann-sandra.com)* both list a number of club links.

MAKE A PLAYDATE

www.singleshikes.com

Singles scene getting you down? Stop barhopping and start trail blazing. If you live in Boulder, Colorado, you can join scheduled hikes with Boulder Singles Hikes. Arizona singles can find a lot of outdoor clubs and singles organizations at 2AZ *(www.2az.us)*. There's love on the East Coast, too. New Jersey's Harriman Hikers club *(www.harrimanhikers.org)* has been organizing singles hikes for thirty years. The Bay Area Jewish Singles

Hiking Club *(www.bajshc.org)* organizes hiking and cycling outings to Big Sur, Big Basin Redwoods State Park, San Francisco, and other areas.

NS HWP HIKER SEEKS SAME
www.fitness-singles.com

Men seeking women or men, and women seeking men or women, can all look for love or a hiking partner at Fitness Singles. You have to register to read the profiles, but you can view the photos for free. Just click on an outdoor activity, and you're ready to seek. If you're looking for group outings, try Meetup *(www.meetup.com)*, where you can look for hiking, walking, biking, and other outdoor-related groups in your area.

OUT IN THE OUTDOORS
www.gayoutdoors.org

Gay Outdoors is the answer, whether you want to connect with gay skiers in the Chicago area, hang with the fellows at Nude Dudes in Arizona, or go caving with gay, lesbian, and bisexual adventurers in Pennsylvania. Read destination articles, trip reports, and outdoor news; look for regional clubs and nude swimming holes; join kayaking and hiking chats; and meet new friends. The daily photo is always a mystery—will it be a nature shot...or a hot, shirtless guy?

NORTHWEST NATIVE
www.mountaineers.org

The one-hundred-year-old Mountaineers organization, based in Seattle, offers courses in backpacking and hiking, avalanche awareness, climbing, kayaking, first aid, leadership, photography, winter sports, and even folk dancing. They also organize outdoor outings, including singles events. It's not all fun and games in the backcountry. The Mountaineers take conservation seriously and are always looking for volunteers to write letters to Congress and get involved in stewardship projects.

THE ORIGINAL OUTDOOR CLUB
www.outdoors.org

Founded in 1876, the Appalachian Mountain Club is the oldest outdoor organization in the country. With chapters across the mid-Atlantic, the

AMC offers thousands of trips a year, from day hikes and paddles to extended backpacking and camping adventures. They also offer a variety of educational programs and volunteer opportunities. Not all the volunteer jobs involve manual labor—you could get a cush job like monitoring alpine flowers or helping out with an air quality study.

ROCKY MOUNTAIN "HI!"
www.cmc.org
Backpacking, hiking, ice skating, rock climbing, camping, and volleyball are just a few of the group activities you can enjoy with other members of the Colorado Mountain Club. The CMC also organizes some cool adventure trips, such as trekking in New Zealand, hiking with llamas to Escalante Canyon, and admiring the rhododendrons in Bhutan. When you get back from your trip, it's time to give back. You'll have your choice of volunteer jobs: repairing trails, picking up garbage, or erosion control.

PLAY, PRESERVE, AND PROTECT
www.sierrraclub.org
Never travel alone again! The Sierra Club offers more than 350 outdoor vacation packages. Explore ancient ruins in Guatemala, swim with dolphins in the Florida Keys, or cycle the Oregon coast. Or take a lower-priced volunteer vacation and help maintain and construct trails, assist with archaeology projects, and repair alpine meadows in parks around the country. There are more than one hundred chapters nationally, so there's a good chance you can find plenty of day outings close to home, too. Of course, the Sierra Club is a big player in conservation issues, so click to the Inside Sierra Club and Take Action sections to see what they're doing to save the planet and how you can help.

29 WOMEN'S WORLD

THESE BABES ROCK

www.babesinthebackcountry.com

These babes get around. So can you with a few classes under your belt. Go to a Snow Divas camp in British Columbia to learn backcountry telemark skills and avalanche safety; attend a Spokeswomen single-track mountain bike weekend in Utah or California; or check out one of the Babes' rock climbing clinics. Babes in the Backcountry also offers summer and winter workshops, classes and retreats, and a summer ski trip to Chile. Check out their hut-to-hut trips, too.

WOMEN WHO WANDER

www.journeywoman.com

Follow your sistas through their travel tales and read about a purse-snatching baboon in South Africa, a menstruation ceremony in Bali, and packing disposable clothing for a European bike tour. Journey Woman is a friendly online resource for women travelers of all ages, with articles and tips on safety, health, spas, and dealing with long flights. Check the city guides for urban adventures. Journey Woman also may have the world's most comprehensive, if not only, International Dim Sum Directory.

ANSWER THE CALL

www.callwild.com

Don't wait around for others; just go! You'll always find women to hike with at Call of the Wild. They've been leading women's wilderness and travel adventure trips for almost thirty years. Sometimes the call leads to wildflower or autumn leaves hikes in Tahoe, sometimes to trekking to Machu Picchu, swimming with dolphins in New Zealand, snowshoeing in the High Sierra, or backpacking in the Grand Canyon. Trips are rated from easy to challenging, so you can choose how hard you want to work. Call of the Wild also designs custom trips for groups.

LEARN IT, LIVE IT
www.uwsp.edu/cnr/bow

Maybe you're not as adventurous as you'd like to be. That's okay. You're not alone. More than twenty thousand women have learned outdoor skills through Becoming an Outdoors-Woman programs offered in forty states. Check the course schedule for classes and events near you; most are offered by state natural resources departments. Learn canoeing skills, outdoor survival techniques, orienteering, tracking, and more.

UP IN THE AIR
Hang out with the ladies at **Women's Climbing** (www.womenclimbing.com) for women's climbing achievements, quotes from pro climbers, and lots of links to like-minded sites. Visit PBS for coverage of the first all-women Sherpa Everest summit (www.pbs.org/frontlineworld/stories/nepal), and view a clip of **Trailblazing: The Women of Nepal's Trekking Industry** at www.trailblazing.ca.

CAPITAL CAMPAIGN
www.washingtonwomenoutdoors.org

You don't have to live in Washington, D.C., to like Washington Women Outdoors. Their Outdoor Internet Resources section is a great resource for guide services, park and trail information, eco travel sites, women-specific outdoor sites, and other trip planning sources. Don't miss the Wildside Adventures link (www.wildsideadventures.com). They offer rock climbing, backpacking, hiking, camping, and kayaking trips for beginners, divas, and everyone in between. They also offer women's retreats, and links to other women's adventure guides, such as Canyon Calling *(www.canyoncalling.com)*. And, if you happen to live in the D.C. area, WWO can keep you busy year-round with hot-air ballooning, hiking, and cross-country skiing outings.

ON THE ROCKS
www.sheclimbs.org
www.womenclimbersnw.org
www.womenswilderness.org

It started in the usual way—a group of women got together and then decided to get more women together. The result? SheClimbs, a grassroots organization dedicated to "putting women on the rocks." Join them for Chicks on Cracks, Goddesses on Cracks, and other climbing get-togethers around the country. The site is a little sparse, but you can always submit a climbing event and ideas for improvement. The links page leads to climbing guides, organizations, and women's outdoor sites such as Women Climbers NW and the Women's Wilderness Institute.

QUEEN OF COOL
www.yourexpedition.com

In my book, nobody kicks ass more than Ann Bancroft (not the actress, although she rocked hard in her day, too). She's half my size and skied across Antarctica pulling a two-hundred-pound sled on the first women-only crossing of the continent. She was the first woman to travel to the North Pole as part of the Will Steger Expedition in 1986, and the first to reach both poles. Bancroft shares her expeditions with schoolchildren via her Dare To Dream curricula and with adults via public lectures and motivational speeches to corporate bosses. Get inspired reading past expedition press releases, viewing the photo gallery, and scanning past interviews to soak up Ann's one-foot-in-front-of-the-other philosophy. Sweet.

WOMAN WALKING
www.oneearthadventures.com

When most retired folks are content to join AARP and plan luxury vacations, explorer Helen Thayer, usually accompanied by her husband Bill, takes long walks across some of the world's most brutal terrains. The first woman to solo either pole when she walked alone with her Inuit dog Charlie to the magnetic North Pole in 1988 at age fifty, Thayer has crossed the Gobi and Sahara deserts and the Canadian Yukon, trekked to both poles, and kayaked 1200 miles along the Amazon River. Thayer's no-nonsense approach to exploration is a refreshing alternative in the often testosterone-drenched adventure world. Her journal entries from current and archived adventures are here, along with photos and articles on cultures and animal species encountered along the way.

WOMEN ARE NOT SMALL MEN
www.outdoordivas.com

Shop and learn at Outdoor Divas, an online store for women. Visit their blog first to meet a few divas: Susan Holden Walsh is a public relations professional who volunteers for a trails maintenance organization in Colorado. Nadia Kimmel, founder of Desert Mountain Medicine, teaches women wilderness and survival skills. And of course, there's Divas' founder Kim Wlaker. Visit the Divas blog for gear news and links to sport training and conditioning info. When you're through, fill your virtual shopping bag with Terry bicycle apparel, Five Ten climbing shoes, and trail pants from Sierra Designs and Ex Officio. You'll find all the top women's brands here.

ONE LUMP OR TWO?
www.wombats.org

I have to admit I expected more from the Wombats Women's Mountain Bike & Tea Society…like a tea cake recipe or at least some tea making tips. Maybe that's a members-only thing. Instead, find a selection of tips on choosing a bike, what constitutes mountain biking "fashion," and trailside manners, as well as a catalog of Wombats "schwag," or logo wear, with fun vintage-inspired graphics. There's also a ride rating system, club ride schedules and events, international mountain biking excursions, and links to cycling resources. Maybe it's time for more Wombats branches. Start one in your city; the ride-and-sip concept has already spread from its San Francisco roots to Massachusetts, New Mexico, and Alaska.

30 A DOG'S DAY OUT

LEASH YOUR LASSIE
www.sierraclub.org

Sure, it's fun to watch your dog romp around in the woods or play in the surf, but don't forget about the native animals in the area. Curious canines can easily disrupt their lives and habitats. In fact, dogs aren't allowed on national park or national monument trails. Before you go, visit the E-Files section of the Sierra Club site for basic guidelines on taking dogs with you into the outdoors. Also, check pet regulations for specific parks at the National Park Service *(www.nps.gov)*.

TRAIL TERRIERS
www.uberpest.com

Pack out the poop? Yes. Pack on the pooch? Definitely. Your dog needs to prepare for adventures as much as you do, and by the way, why should you get all the fun gear? Read about outfitting and caring for your dog on the trail at UberPest's Journal. The Dog Hiking FAQs and articles cover basic first aid, conditioning and training, trail etiquette, and special considerations for hot and cold weather hiking. There's also a list of canine first-aid items recommended by the Red Cross. Take a minute to meet UberPest's pets, Lucy, Beau, and Stuffy. Also worth a visit are the Hiking With Your Dog and Camping With Your Dog tips at Love the Outdoors *(www.lovetheoutdoors.com)* and the hiking and backpacking tips at K9 Trailblazers *(www.k9trailblazers.org)*.

DOG DAY AFTERNOON
www.hikewithyourdog.com
So your dog's not welcome in some parks? Big deal. Get online and find dog-friendly trails at Hike With Your Dog. In addition to trail listings and links, the site sells books and pamphlets on dog regulations for hundreds of U.S. trails, parks, and beaches. There are also some useful safety articles. For instance, did you know that your dog can roll in poison ivy without an itch, but he can pass it to you? Don't forget to check your pooch for ticks post-hike. Also visit Dogpark.com *(www.dogpark.com)* to find a dog park in your area.

HAVE DOG, WILL TRAVEL
www.dogfriendly.com
Dogs like to get away sometimes, too. A hike is nice, but a road trip is even better. For many Fidos, cross-country skiing is the ultimate treat. Dog-Friendly won't win Best in Show designwise, but it has listings and links to hotels, campgrounds, RV parks, beaches, resorts, and even rental car companies that accommodate pets and their owners. There's also travel-specific information on customs and quarantine laws, air travel, beach and travel etiquette, pet-friendly hotel chains, and dog regulations for public transportation. TravelDog *(www.traveldog.com)* and TakeYourPet *(www.takeyourpet.com)* offer similar content, both with much more attractive design formats, on a subscription basis.

DOG PADDLING
www.dogpaddlingadventures.com
You don't always have to think of everything. The folks at Dog Paddling Adventures in Ontario have some fun trips planned for you and your dog. They'll provide gear and meals; you just bring the dog food. Go canoeing and camping in the summer, hiking in the spring and fall, and skijoring and snowshoeing in the winter. If you think your dog won't stay in the boat, they say he will. Just in case, they have a life jacket in his size.

WORK LIKE A DOG

http://channel.nationalgeographic.com
/channel/programs/dogs-with-jobs.html

So your dog has a hero complex. Let him learn more about the life of a search-and-rescue dog before you pooh-pooh the idea. National Geographic's popular television series, *Dogs with Jobs*, features working dogs on the job, such as the nimble Nyak, an Irish setter circus performer; Buddy, a sheltie service dog who works with children; and Cinder, a Belgian malinois police dog doing her best to take a bite out of crime. Visit the site to watch the show's promo video, featuring Part-Ex, the surfing, kayaking, rock climbing extreme sports dog (and Guinness World Record holder), and view the photo gallery of more working dogs. See, you can teach an old dog new tricks.

THE PROUD, THE FEW

www.dogscouts.com

Just because your dog always seems happy to see you doesn't mean she's happy. Maybe she has dreams, too. Maybe she'd like a chance to be all she can be. Dog Scouts of America might be the perfect place for her. She can learn how to play Frisbee or train to be a sled dog. If she's really motivated, she can earn merit badges in hiking, biking, backpacking, letterboxing and geocaching, obstacle courses, water safety, tracking, and other outdoor and service categories. She can even start her own troop, and she doesn't have to sell cookies to go to camp. Dog Scouts does not discriminate: all well-mannered dogs are welcome, regardless of gender, sexual orientation, or religious disbeliefs.

PLAYDATES FOR POOCHES

www.skijor.org

If you and your dog are bored with tossing the tennis ball, it's time to break out of your rut and find some new sports. Skijoring is a lot of fun, and a lot easier than mushing. Just strap on your nordic skis and let your dog pull you through the snow. In warmer months, take it to the streets on a skateboard, scooter, cart, or bicycle *(www.dogscooter.com)*. If your dog would rather ride the skateboard than pull it, check out the website of Tyson, the skateboarding bulldog *(www.skateboardingbulldog.com)*.

ANOTHER DAY, ANOTHER DOG

www.dogster.com

Do you and your dog ever feel like there's something missing in your relationship? Dogs get bored, too. They think about running through the forest alone, no leash, no commitments. They think about what it would be like to find love, true love, at the dog park. What about you? Are you even sure you're a one-dog person? Maybe it's time for both of you to scratch that itch. At Dogster, you can discuss all of your dog issues with other owners and even set up playdates. Your dog can post her own website, learn a few new tricks, and network with other dogs. By the time you both finish viewing the puppy photo gallery, you'll be ready to click to the travel section to find dog-friendly hotels for your next trip.

STEWARDSHIP AND SUSTAINABLE LIVING

I think the environment should be put in the category of our national security. Defense of our resources is just as important as defense abroad. Otherwise what is there to defend?

— Robert Redford

31 PRESERVE AND PROTECT

KEEP IT CLEAN; KEEP IT GREEN
www.lnt.org

Don't lace up your boots until you know the seven Leave No Trace Principles. It's very simple: respect the land (that includes the trees, the plants, the animals, the water) and fellow hikers. It's easier to prevent destruction than repair it. The nonprofit Leave No Trace Center for Outdoor Ethics offers a variety of skills and awareness programs for adults and children. Spread the message; become a member.

SAVE THE BATS
www.batcon.org

Everyone wants to save the whales. They're massive, majestic, mythical. And cheetahs. How sexy are they, with their speckled fur and 0 to 60 mph acceleration? But if you really want to feel virtuous, try saving an animal that totally creeps you out. Bats get a bad rap, but we need them to eat all those West Nile virus–carrying mosquitoes. Really, bats are just trying to save our lives. Cut them some slack and get involved. Nobody's asking you to touch them; just support them. Learn more about the bats in your belfry, as well as bat natural history and other issues at Bat Conservation International. Send a bat ecard, submit a bat poem, and build a bat house in your yard. The site also has links to bat-related articles and research papers, and even audio files of bat chat.

POOPER TROOPERS
www.haddusa.com

Stop pooping on public trails! Yeah, you. And your dog, too. The members of Hikers Against Doo-Doo are steaming mad, and they're taking their Faex-Free Trail campaign on the road. Their site isn't extensive, but rest assured, their leader, pathologist Dr. Bern Hoff, "truly knows his shit." Aren't you tired of putting up with other people's crap? Join HADD, and you'll get free "No Doo-Doo" stickers and a deed to one square inch of feces-free land in Maine. HADD also sells a limited range of products, including blueprints for a traditional outhouse.

32 NEWS AND VIEWS

TOTALLY FRESH
www.grist.org
Environmental news doesn't have to be as dry as day-old gluten-free toast.
There's plenty of jam to go around at Grist, where daily features might
include an article about a "green" skateboard manufacturer, an interview
with the owner of an eco-friendly laundromat, reviews of books about air,
tear-jerking environmental movies, and a recyclable museum. Ask cranky
columnist Umbra Fisk for advice on green living, discuss articles with
like-minded readers on the Gristmill blog, and check live feeds for daily
news. Smart, witty, and wise, this is my favorite online magazine.

FASHIONABLY GREEN
www.treehugger.com
With more than six thousand archived articles, plus reader-submitted
news alerts, Treehugger covers a lot of green ground on its hip lifestyle
site: designer handbags made from preworn business suits, a bike made
out of wood, Malcom Gladwell's views on alternative energy sources,
organic cotton high-tops, build-it-yourself wooden kayak kits, celebrity-
on-a-bike sightings, green roof vs. solar panel, eco-gifts under $50. Plus,
you'll find a green job board, and a design contest to find sustainable
everyday products and couture from reused materials. If not for Treehugger, I also might never have found out about the Ditty Bops, a quirky,
multitalented musical duo with the cutest, coolest website ever *(www.
thedittybops.com)*, who ride to their gigs on mountain bikes.

E FOR ENVIRONMENTAL

www.emagazine.com

Straight-up and action-oriented, *E* magazine always includes source links with every feature article and EarthTalk column, so readers can dig a little deeper into their favorite topics. *E*'s news and commentaries follow key "e" issues—from climate change to ecotourism to tree-free paper. Search the site for "hiking" and the list of related topics may include travel pieces about Yosemite or Canada, consumer news about low-impact outdoor gear, or a feature story on women's leadership in the environmental movement. There's a lot to read for free, but you need a subscription to see it all. *E* is also available as a bimonthly paper magazine printed on recycled paper, but why not stick to enews and reduce demand for paper?

GET ON THE NETWORK

www.enn.com

Follow dozens of pro-earth organizations—from the Sea Turtle Restoration Project to the Earth Policy Institute—and daily news feeds on water, energy, wildlife, and sustainability topics from Reuters and the Associated Press at one convenient location, the Environmental News Network. The site also provides commentary by environmental leaders and scientists such as Dr. David Suzuki *(www.davidsuzuki.org)*, as well as an online bulletin board with job, event, and workshop listings. If you don't want to be deskbound, you can listen to ENN's radio news and interviews or download free podcasts.

33 TAKE ACTION

GET INVOLVED
www.nrdc.org

Everything I need to know to save the planet, I learned at the Natural Resources Defense Council website. Superbly organized in an easy-to-navigate newsletter format, the site's loaded with information and options. Read a quick overview of water pollution; pore over in-depth reports and white papers on climate issues; or watch *Lethal Sounds*, a five-minute video about the damage whales suffer from man-made noise, narrated by sexy Pierce Brosnan (Robert Redford and James Taylor are on the NRDC board of trustees). Most important, the NRDC site is designed to inspire action—yours! Click on Take Action at the top of every page to visit the Earth Action Center, where you can send prewritten messages to Washington (or write your own), learn about action tips and tools, and even track your action profile. If animals are your thing, click on the Biogems image for quick info on how to the help Florida's turtles, California's whales, or Yellowstone's buffalo. There's also a kids' page.

NO MORE EXCUSES
www.lcv.org

You'd write to your senator about global warming, but you just don't have the time to look up her address. No more excuses; visit the League of Conservation Voters site now, and get involved. Type in your zip code, and in seconds you'll have profiles of your state and U.S. senators and representatives, including their committees, and links to their email addresses. LCV makes it easy to check up on how the president, environmental agencies, and Congress are handling key issues. Track LCV press releases, as well as the latest environmental news from Washington, or be really lazy and sign up for email alerts.

34 GETTING GREEN

LIVELY UP YOURSELF
www.voiceyourself.com

It's not just about hemp for actor and eco-activist Woody Harrelson and his wife, Laura Louie—it's about transforming the world. Their colorful, informative site, Voice Yourself, has a refreshingly personal approach to promoting planet-friendly living, with a list of recommended "desert island" reading (Michael Moore's *Stupid White Men*, John Robbins' *The Food Revolution*, and T. K. V. Desikachar's *The Heart of Yoga*, to name a few), reader-submitted poems, and personal tributes. There's plenty of news, too, sourced from Grist.org, *E* magazine, the *New York Times,* and any other publication with a worthwhile article or commentary. Learn how to "Leave a Lighter Footprint," take action on current environmental campaigns, and submit your nominees for Earth Shaper and Earth Raper of the month.

LIVING GREEN
www.thegreenguide.com

Before you buy that mattress or eat that mercury-laden fish, you might want to check *The Green Guide*, the *Consumer Reports* for the planet- and health-conscious. You'll need a subscription for full access to current and archived online News and Views articles, product warnings, and recommendations. After you read an article, you have options: print it, buy it, click to related news stories, or email it to a friend. Even if you don't subscribe, you can receive a free weekly enewsletter, read product-related blogs with emailable posts, and visit the site's message board, aka The Green Gab, where members rate, rank, rave, and rant about organic chocolate, eco-friendly shampoos and deodorants, natural insect repellents, and more.

NOT IN MY NEIGHBORHOOD
www.scorecard.org

Wouldn't you like to know exactly who's polluting your little space on Earth, not to mention your neighbor's space and your brother's space, and everywhere in between? Scorecard can tell you. Just type in your zip code, and you can find out about toxic chemicals in the local water, air, and dirt, and who put them there. You can also learn, by income and race, who lives in Superfund sites and cancer-risk zones. Kinda gives you something to think about, so you'll want to go to the mother site, Environmental Defense *(www.environmentaldefense.org)*, for the latest news, press releases, and campaigns. Their action pages tell you how and why to make personal changes that benefit the planet (and, in fact, have a sign-in pledge form to encourage you to make those changes). Get your friends involved, too. They provide a pre-written email form you can send to Washington. Easy.

FAST TALKERS
http://greenlagirl.com

You don't have to live in Los Angeles to love Green LA Girl's highly caffeinated fair trade blog, but you might need a cuppa java to keep up with her. Read the Coffee Crisis Series, then get all interactive and take the Starbucks Challenge. If chocolate's your poison, you'll enjoy following LA Girl's fair trade chocolate tasting parties. No news feeds here, just opinions (and thoughtful reader feedback). LA Girl also links to her favorite eco-finds, online and otherwise, such as vegan knitting, the 100 Mile Diet, and a cycling site that helps riders find routes and calculate the carbon dioxide pollutants they'll prevent (not to mention the calories they'll burn) along the way. Plus links to lots of other cool sites, such as fiftyRx3 *(http://fiftyrx3.blogspot.com)*, a sustainable-fashion blog, and LA Green Living *(www.lagreenliving.com)*, an online resource for Southern California.

WASTE NOT
www.reduce.org

The average American office worker uses 10,000 sheets of paper a year. Then there's junk mail; 4.3 tons of it ends up in the garbage every year. How many pounds of garbage do you create every day? How about taking a pledge to reduce and conserve? You can do just that at the Minnesota Pollution Control Agency website. Even if you don't live in the Land of 10,000 Lakes, visit this site for easy-to-manage tips highlighting simple actions you can take to reduce waste in your life. Learn how to make non-toxic household cleaners, maintain a waste-free lawn, and stay eco while traveling and during holidays.

HAVE YOU PLANTED A TREE TODAY?
www.arborday.org

Long before there was Earth Day, there was Arbor Day. Grab a shovel and visit the National Arbor Day Foundation's site for info on Arbor Day tree-planting celebrations in 10 U.S. cities. (FYI, National Arbor Day is the last Friday in April, but many states celebrate it on different dates determined by optimal planting conditions.) Browse the tree guide, brush up on tree vocabulary, and review the list of "9 Things You Should Know About Trees." For more in-depth information, watch tree-planting videos or chat with other tree people in the forum. When you're ready for action, check out the foundation's many programs, purchase trees for yourself or as a gift, or volunteer to plant a tree. If you're looking for a way to procrastinate at work, the tree identification guide will keep you busy until retirement—and if you get caught surfing it, you can say you were just trying to save a tree.

THE MARCH ONLINE
www.stopglobalwarming.org

Would you rather read a news report on using soybean oil in your car or watch Willie Nelson talk about it? Yeah, me, too. Don't feel guilty; inspiration is where it starts. The Stop Global Warming Virtual March, now 500,000 people strong, wants you to learn it, share it, and mobilize, and if they can entertain you along the way, even better. This interactive activist site will get you fired up about the climate crisis, with a variety of video calls to action featuring Al Gore, Robert F. Kennedy, and actor Jack Black, among others. Don't miss the SpongeBob SquarePants video on global warming or Will Ferrell's impersonation of George Bush trying to sound like he cares about the environment. Check out photos and environmental statements of famous "marchers" Senator Barack Obama, Walter Cronkite, Bonnie Raitt, Jon Bon Jovi, skateboarder Tony Hawk, and dozens more. Stay current with environmental news feeds, and pester your mayor to join the Climate Protection Act (if he or she hasn't already). Finally, visit Willie's biodiesel site *(www.wnbiodiesel.com)*.

GREASE IS GOOD
www.thebiggreenbus.org

Go ahead and order the fries: the kids on The Big Green Bus can fill up their tank with the used oil. For the past two summers, a small group of Dartmouth students has taken their "change your fuel, change the world" message on the road, crisscrossing the country in a green, veggie-powered bus. Their itinerary includes stops at environmental fairs, outdoor concerts, and ultimate Frisbee tournaments—although it's not always clear from their trip journals and photos what their outreach presentations entail. Still, they deserve credit for trying and for volunteering along the way, doing mold removal duty in Biloxi, Mississippi, for HandsOn Gulf Coast. With high-profile sponsors such as Newman's Own, Annie's Homegrown, Whole Foods Markets, and Clif Bar, the bus is sure to be back on the road next year.

GET IN GEAR, VOLUNTEER
www.americanhiking.org/policy/current

You can learn a lot about trail ecology, conservation, policy, and volunteerism at The American Hiking Society site. Start with the Current Issues page for policy and legislation information, and find out if your state representatives are members of the House Trails Caucus. Now you're ready for action. The AHS makes it easy for you to send a prewritten message to Congress (you can personalize the message or write your own) with just a few clicks. When you're ready to get your hands dirty, click on your state to find volunteer vacations and National Trails Day events in your area. Once you've done your part, you can also search the site for hikes and hiking tips.

THE LONG TRAIL

www.greenmountainclub.org

Vermont's Long Trail is the oldest long-distance trail in the United States. At 270 miles with 175 side trails, it's also a lot of work to maintain. That's why the Green Mountain Club was formed. With nine thousand members and eight hundred active volunteers, the club organizes trail repair events and teaches low-impact hiking skills. Take a working vacation and help rejuvenate a trail, or join them for classes and workshops on hiking, snowshoeing, mountaineering, and more.

GEAR

There is no such thing as bad weather, only inappropriate clothing.

—Sir Ranulph Fiennes

35 WHAT TO WEAR

GET YOUR GEAR ON
www.fitnesstravelgear.com

Before you spend $250 on a new soft shell jacket, wouldn't it be nice to know more about it? Fitness Travel Gear features hands-on, personality-driven reviews of outdoor, fitness, and travel products. The review team consists of several outdoor writers and editors, as well as competitive athletes. To name a few: Joe, an author and a former Olympic kayaker, is an expert on outdoor apparel that won't smell after use; Daniel bikes 50 miles to work every day and knows his way around all types of technical fabrics; and Erika (I give; that's me) is obsessed with quality footwear, merino wool, and iPod accessories. Naturally, FTG, which is updated monthly, is well written and the reviews are comprehensive yet concise. Denali, the site's dog mascot, voices opinions about doggie gear in her own column, Ask Denali. Click from reviews to manufacturer's sites and shopping links.

GUY STUFF
www.gearreview.com

Looking for new pedals for your mountain bike, Gore-Tex waders, or snowboard bindings? The guys at GearReview probably have recommendations for each item. Search by manufacturer or by activity and read comprehensive comparative assessments. Just don't expect to find many sports bra reviews here; with the exception of a few female guest reviewers, the majority of apparel and footwear is tested by men.

You can find good sales on men's, women's, and children's gear in the shopping section. Reviews include links to manufacturers' sites.

WHAT TO WEAR
www.worldclassgear.com

In addition to field-tested reviews of hiking and travel apparel and footwear in a clean, easy-to-browse format, World Class Gear has a few useful packing guide charts for adventure travel, mountaineering, and hiking. Each essential item includes an explanation of how or why to use the product, plus at least one link to a relevant product review. Some reviews are written in feature article format, describing testing locations, with links to explanations of the gear used. Search for reviews by activity or by manufacturer, or sign up to receive an email alert whenever new reviews are posted.

SWAP MEET
www.trailspace.com

Trailspace features reader-submitted reviews of hiking, backpacking, and camping gear. You might find seven reviews of a particular pack or jacket, or only one. Some reviews contain basic product descriptions from other sites and online retailers; all items are ranked by a 1–5 star system (1 = not so great, 5 = must have), and all reviews include shopping links. Check the forum to swap backcountry tips and shop for or sell used gear. The staff-written buying guides for packs, tents, and other items are also worth a look. Get a peek at next season's gear in the industry news section.

ADDICTION WITHOUT A CURE
www.thegearjunkie.com

Stephen Regenold doesn't just test gear, he takes it on full-blown expeditions. As a freelance travel writer, he has skied deep in the Canadian wilderness, explored canyons in Utah, and paddled, trekked, and climbed his way through a 417-mile desert obstacle course. Read about his trips in the features section, or sit back and watch the video clips and slideshows. When you're ready to find out what he wore, click to the gear archives for reviews of jackets, boots, mountain bikes, flashlights, ice axes, and more.

ALPINE ADVICE

http://alpinistmountainstandards.blogs.com

When you're dangling off the edge of an ice face, you need to know your gear is up to the job. Who better to trust than the "guides, semipros, and dirtbags" at Alpinist Mountain Standards, the gear blog of *Alpinist* magazine? Check out the men and women on the Review Panel on the bio pages, then dig in. The reviews are energetic and fun to read, covering a variety of ice and rock climbing products.

36 WHERE TO SHOP

REI
www.rei.com

Need a few essentials? REI has base layers from SmartWool; Ex Officio travel clothes; outerwear by Mountain Hardwear, Marmot, the North Face, and Arc'Teryx; Eagle Creek luggage and accessories; packs from Jansport, Gregory, and Osprey; and casual wear from Columbia, Royal Robbins, Gramicci, and Prana. Gear up here for backpacking and camping trips, paddling and cycling adventures, and more. In addition to stocking a variety of well-known brands, REI sells its own signature label apparel and packs. Check for deals during semiannual sales and at the REI outlet site *(www.rei-outlet.com)*. Members earn yearly dividends on selected purchases. The best part of the REI site may be the Expert Advice section, where you'll find detailed articles and tips on every topic from selecting the right tent to planning a bike tour to water safety tips for paddlers. Don't miss these articles! REI has more than ninety stores in twenty-six states; check the site for classes, workshops, and trips.

ALTREC
www.altrec.com

Altrec has free shipping on orders over $45, and they pay postage on returns. Nice. You'll find popular outdoor brands such as Mountain Hardwear, Outdoor Research, Patagonia, Arc'Teryx, the North Face, Osprey, Sierra Designs, Salomon, Pearl Izumi, and Jetboil. This store's not just for hikers; there's plenty of paddling gear by NRS and Kokatat, as well as boards and apparel by Burton, Roxy, and Billabong. Altrec has a good selection of footwear brands, including Merrell, Salomon, Montrail, Nike, and Keen. Check the outlet section for post-season deals.

US OUTDOOR STORE

www.usoutdoorstore.com

At US Outdoor Store you can buy a wakeboard, a snowboard, a watch, an ice ax, a bikini, a tent, or just about anything else you'd need to have fun on land, snow, or water. Shipping is free on orders over $40. They stock dozens of popular (and many lesser-known) brands, including Giro, Black Diamond, Kavu, Leki, Five Ten, Snozu, and Tubbs. Note: the prices in the closeout section don't seem low enough to me, but maybe you have to keep checking for reductions.

MOOSEJAW

www.moosejaw.com

The wacky guys at Moosejaw are all about spreading the love and making it fun to shop. In the Moosejaw Madness section you can view photos of people wearing Moosejaw T-shirts on mountains, in the woods, on sailboats, and at other outdoorsy vacation spots. If you're bored and lonely, email Dating Girl for relationship advice, check out employee iPod playlists, or click on a number of other interactive options. Or you can shop for hiking, camping, climbing, and snowboarding gear. They carry Outdoor Research, Merrell, Montrail, Patagonia, Kelty, Mountainsmith, Water Girl, Chaco, Suunto, and many other brands. Free shipping on orders over $49, plus frequent shopping rewards points! Moosejaw has two retail stores in Michigan and one in Illinois.

CAMPMOR

www.campmor.com

Here are the kinds of bargains you'll find at Campmor: a Marmot jacket for $59.97 (reg. $100), Montrail women's hiking boots for $79.96 (reg. $129.99), and a $70 pair of Smith sunglasses for under $30. Shop for all sports and all seasons. Campmor has every imaginable piece of apparel, gadget, and equipment. They make it easy for your loved ones to shop for you with a gift registry; you can also email friends and family pages of your favorite items. Check the links page for camping, hiking, and cycling sites, as well as outdoor magazines and clubs. Campmor has a bricks-and-mortar store in New Jersey (see the website for the GPS coordinates).

SIERRA TRADING POST
www.sierratradingpost.com
For great deals on apparel and footwear, visit Sierra Trading Post. They buy out-of-season and overstock items from hundreds of vendors, and sell it for 35–75 percent off suggested retail prices. Save 49 percent on a Mountain Hardwear jacket, 65 percent on Scarpa hiking boots, and 41 percent on a Cloudveil wicking top. Visit the Bargain Barn for $30 Brooks running shoes and $48 Rossignol ski boots. Start your gear search here if you want more for less.

EASTERN MOUNTAIN SPORTS
www.ems.com
Eastern Mountain Sports deserves some respect and attention. As a store, they may not be as well-known as REI, and as a brand they don't have the name recognition of Patagonia or Columbia, but their gear is just as attractive, functional, and durable as any of the top brands. I've personally wear-tested several of their signature brand items, including a rain jacket, rain pants, and a fleece jacket, and recommend them all. At the online store you'll find apparel, footwear, and all sorts of gear for paddling, hiking, cycling, climbing, skiing, and travel. You'll also find plenty of big names, such as SmartWool, Teva, Nalgene, Atlas, MSR, La Sportiva, and Leatherman. Read the boot-fitting guide before you shop for footwear. EMS offers courses in climbing and kayaking, as well as adventure trips and treks to India, Nepal, Costa Rica, and other exotic destinations. Visit during the Labor Day sale to save up to 70 percent.

BACKCOUNTRY
www.backcountry.com
If there's a trail involved or mountains of snow, Backcountry has the goods to go. Shop for North Face packs, Highgear altimeters, Yakima roof racks, fat skis, skinny skis, wicking shirts by Helly Hansen, Sugoi, and Patagonia, down jackets, Gore-Tex jackets, and soft shell jackets.

Backcountry sells paddling gear, too. You can compare similar products with a few clicks, view a list of top selling items, and scan reader-submitted gear reviews. There's no shipping charge for items over $50, and you can find half-off sales in the outlet section. Don't shop so hard you miss the Backcountry blog.

L.L.BEAN
www.llbean.com

Still the best place to buy a flannel shirt or a cotton turtleneck, but there's more. L.L.Bean still sells a no-frills flannel-lined sleeping bag, but they also sell totally compressible, Polarguard-stuffed bags rated to 20°F. Skip the drab casual clothes, and go straight to the Outdoor Gear and Apparel section. You'll find packs by Gregory, the North Face, and Mountainsmith; nordic skis by Karhu and Fischer; spray skirts by Harmony, Advanced Elements, and Pakboats; and a pretty good selection of brand-name apparel and gear for hiking, cycling, and fishing. Make sure to visit the Explore the Outdoors pages for dozens of equipment guides and a list of courses and trips offered by L.L.Bean's Discovery Schools.

MEC
www.mec.ca

Shop in English or Français for Adventure Medical first-aid kits, Garmin GPS units, G3 climbing skins, all types of kayaks and canoes, Sidi cycling shoes, and more at Mountain Equipment Co-Op, the REI of Canada. Like REI, MEC carries popular brands in addition to its own brand. MEC's outdoor apparel is made in Canada using many of the same technical fabrics—such as Polartec's Power Shield and Gore-Tex's Windstopper—you'll find in similar products from more expensive brands. Finding great gear for less isn't even the most exciting feature here—getting tons of free advice is. They'll tell you what to wear, how to select equipment, how to repair equipment, where to go, how to get started, how to stay safe, and what to bring on every sort of outing—from day hikes to white-water kayak trips to ice climbing adventures. MEC has eleven retail stores across Canada and offers an extensive list of outdoor skills courses. This is my favorite online gear store; I can shop, plan, and learn all in one place.

MAGELLAN'S
www.magellans.com

Not just your parents' travel supply shop, Magellan's soothing philosophy is all about comfort, safety, and solving common travel woes. Pick up a doorstop alarm, packing cubes, an in-flight power converter (with continuous power, you can watch all the DVDs you want on your laptop, no matter how long the flight), and the most essential—Bose Noise Canceling Headphones for your iPod. Sit back and enjoy the ride.

LIMMER BOOTS
www.limmerboot.com

These boots were made for walkin'. If you have hard-to-fit feet, or just demand skilled craftsmanship, visit Limmer Boots. Based in New Hampshire, this family-owned enterprise has been making beautiful boots for nearly one hundred years. Their off-the-shelf boots, made in Germany, have garnered rave reviews from the top outdoor magazines. If you want custom boots, get in line. There's a three-year waiting list.

THRU-HIKER
www.thru-hiker.com

Brand-name booty breakin' your bank? DIY, and save a bundle. Thru-Hiker has everything you need to make your own insulated jacket or vest, wind shirt, stuff sack, and tarp tent. Purchase kits for these items (you just stitch them together), or check out The Workshop for a fleece mittens pattern, as well as for illustrated instructions on knee articulation, French seams, and other sewing techniques. Maybe you have your own patterns; Thru-Hiker also sells zippers, cords, down, synthetic insulation, performance fabric, and pre-made shoulder straps. Plus, gear reviews and a message board.

FEATHERED FRIENDS
www.featheredfriends.com

Feathered Friends is all about warmth without the weight. This Seattle-based retailer has been making top-quality down sleeping bags since 1972. They have a huge selection of styles and sizes for various camping conditions and alpine expeditions (they even have a bag rated to –60°F if you're really into winter camping). Feathered Friends also makes down jackets, vests, suits, booties, and comforters. You can view their line on the website, then order via phone, fax, or email.

INDEX

ABOUT THE AUTHOR

Erika Dillman is an avid hiker, a yoga teacher, and the author of nine books. She has written numerous articles, and produced radio and online programming, for a variety of national outdoor, fitness, and travel-related publications. Ms. Dillman also produces an online gear guide, *www .fitnesstravelgear.com.*

THE MOUNTAINEERS, founded in 1906, is a nonprofit outdoor activity and conservation club, whose mission is "to explore, study, preserve, and enjoy the natural beauty of the outdoors...." Based in Seattle, Washington, the club is now the third-largest such organization in the United States, with seven branches throughout Washington State.

The Mountaineers sponsors both classes and year-round outdoor activities in the Pacific Northwest, which include hiking, mountain climbing, ski-touring, snowshoeing, bicycling, camping, kayaking, nature study, sailing, and adventure travel. The club's conservation division supports environmental causes through educational activities, sponsoring legislation, and presenting informational programs.

All club activities are led by skilled, experienced instructors, who are dedicated to promoting safe and responsible enjoyment and preservation of the outdoors.

If you would like to participate in these organized outdoor activities or the club's programs, consider a membership in The Mountaineers. For information and an application, write or call The Mountaineers, Club Headquarters, 300 Third Avenue West, Seattle, WA 98119; 206-284-6310. You can also visit the club's website at *www.mountaineers.org* or contact The Mountaineers via email at *clubmail@mountaineers.org*.

The Mountaineers Books, an active, nonprofit publishing program of the club, produces guidebooks, instructional texts, historical works, natural history guides, and works on environmental conservation. All books produced by The Mountaineers Books fulfill the club's mission.

Send or call for our catalog of more than 500 outdoor titles:

The Mountaineers Books
1001 SW Klickitat Way, Suite 201
Seattle, WA 98134
800-553-4453
mbooks@mountaineersbooks.org
www.mountaineersbooks.org

The Mountaineers Books is proud to be a corporate sponsor of The Leave No Trace Center for Outdoor Ethics, whose mission is to promote and inspire responsible outdoor recreation through education, research, and partnerships. The Leave No Trace program is focused specifically on human-powered (nonmotorized) recreation.

Leave No Trace strives to educate visitors about the nature of their recreational impacts, as well as offer techniques to prevent and minimize such impacts. Leave No Trace is best understood as an educational and ethical program, not as a set of rules and regulations.

For more information, visit *www.LNT.org,* or call 800-332-4100.

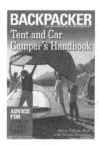